SYMBOLS AND ABBREVIATIONS USED IN T...

C000281418

Good footpath (sufficiently distinct to be followed in mist) -- ...

Intermittent footpath (difficult to follow in mist) ---.---.--.

No path; route recommended ···············.········   Walki...
are no... ...essarily rights of way

Route on motor road   unenclosed   between walls   between fences

Unenclosed road (off route) :::::::::::::::::::::::

Wall ∘∘∘∘∘∘∘∘∘∘   Broken wall ∘∘∘∘∘∘∘   Fence ++++++++++   Broken fence ''''''''''

Limestone clints   Crags   Scree   Boulders

Marshy ground   Trees

Cave or pothole •   Buildings   Contours (at 100' intervals) ········1400···· ········1300····

Summit-cairn ▲   Other (prominent) cairns ⌃   Miles (from starting point) and direction of route ⑤

Stream or river (arrow indicates direction of flow)

Waterfall   Bridge   Railway   Map scale: 2" = 1 mile
North is top of the page

Abbreviations: O.S. Ordnance Survey   Y.H.A Youth Hostels Association

WALKS ON THE HOWGILL FELLS

THE PICTORIAL GUIDES
TO THE
LAKELAND FELLS

Publisher's Note

This book is a re-issue of the original volume written by A. Wainwright. The descriptions of the walks were correct, to the best of A. Wainwright's knowledge, at the time of first publication and are reproduced here without amendment at the wish of the Wainwright Estate. However, since certain footpaths, cairns and other waymarks described here may no longer be accurate, walkers are advised to check with an up-to-date Ordnance Survey map when planning a walk.

A bridge in Langdale

WALKS
ON THE
HOWGILL
FELLS

AND ADJOINING FELLS

AWainwright

PUBLISHED by MICHAEL JOSEPH, LONDON

MICHAEL JOSEPH LTD

Published by the Penguin Group
27 Wrights Lane, London W8, England

Penguin Books Ltd Registered Offices:
Harmondsworth, Middlesex, England

First published by Michael Joseph
1992
Originally published by the Westmorland Gazette, 1972

Printed by Titus Wilson and Son, Kendal

ISBN 0 7181 4010 9

TO

BELL AND MARGARET PRATT

— natives of these parts
who provided much helpful information

*Carved inscription over a doorway
in the Cross Keys Hotel, Cautley:*

GREAT THINGS ARE DONE WHEN MEN AND MOUNTAINS MEET:
THESE ARE NOT DONE BY JOSTLING IN THE STREET.

W. BLAKE

There are three separate and
independent parts to this book
each with its own introduction:

PART ONE
THE WHINFELL RIDGE

THE WHINFELL RIDGE
INTRODUCTION

Between the two roads leaving Kendal for Shap (A.6) and Appleby (A.685), six miles out of the town, there rises an undulating ridge of rough moorland of an average altitude around 1500 feet, surmounted by five distinct summits. The ridge is unpretentious, and indeed dwarfed by higher land nearby; and although seen in its entirety from many parts of Kendal, where it forms the north-east horizon, it has no features to attract particular attention, apart from a recently-erected radio station on the skyline that serves to identify the ridge with certainty in distant views. The ridge is clearly defined by the two roads mentioned, which skirt the flanks, and even better so by the deep trench of Borrowdale 'behind', a lonely and lovely valley; while on the Kendal side the slopes descend less steeply to the headwaters of the River Mint and the fields of a string of farmsteads along the base of the moorland in a pastoral backwater quiet and unspoilt yet within sound and sight of busy roads.

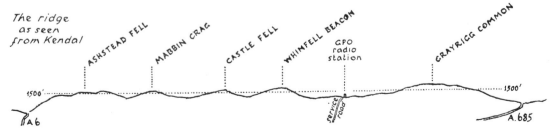

The ridge as seen from Kendal

ASHSTEAD FELL · MABBIN CRAG · CASTLE FELL · WHIMFELL BEACON · GPO radio station · GRAYRIGG COMMON

1500' · 1500'

A.6 · service road · A.685

The ridge forms a watershed between the catchment areas of the Kent (fed by the River Mint) and the Lune (fed by Borrow Beck). The underlying rock is Silurian and although occurring on the surface as low crags in places on the Borrowdale flank is generally covered by peat and moor grass, providing pasturage for sheep and young cattle. There are no cliffs worthy of a rockclimber's attention, but all the fells have rough ground and a few scatterings of boulders facing east and north, and Grayrigg Common has two fine upland combes.   There is little on the ridge to excite botanists but much of interest in the moist pastures of the lower Borrowdale slopes near the foot of the valley, which are well wooded and have some fine specimen trees. Historical associations are lacking although Whinfell Beacon has played a part in notable events down the centuries; but the Romans established an important fort at Low Borrow Bridge near the eastern foot of the ridge: their line of communication with the camp at Watercrook, Kendal, is obscure but may well have crossed the ridge at some point, probably merely as a foot-track.

This tract of high country, lying mostly in the parish of Whinfell, comprises Whinfell Common and Grayrigg Common and may conveniently be referred to as the Whinfell Ridge.

continued

On the map the ridge is five miles long; underfoot the distance seems greater, the hills being more massive than first appearance suggests. From end to end the ridge provides a splendid traverse, free of hazards and with excellent views in all directions: a fine training exercise for a good walker. It is pathless except for sheep tracks and crossed by several walls and a single right of way — an ancient footpath, converted on the Kendal side into a tarmac road to serve the radio station — but there are no prohibitions on access to walkers, who will of course be expected to treat walls and gates with respect.

The ridge is even more enjoyable, however, when explored fully and leisurely in a series of rambles from different starting points, for then not only the ridge but the enclosing valleys will be visited, Borrowdale especially being too fine to miss. Walks 1 to 5 in the following pages are detailed routes that, together, include the main topographical features of the ridge and its approaches.

For readers who nevertheless want to walk the whole ridge from one end to the other at one 'go', the following notes and accompanying diagram are given:

On the A6 at the sharp bend before the descent to Huck's Bridge (travelling north) there is a recessed gate on the east side of the road giving access to a rough cart-track bound for Borrowdale. It is convenient to start the ridgewalk here. Ignore the stony track into Borrowdale and make a beeline for the top of Ashstead Fell in front, thereafter keeping to the height of land all the way and finally descending either direct to the A685 or, more attractively, indirectly to Low Borrow Bridge by way of the foot of Borrowdale. Features of the ridge are shown in detail in Walks 1 to 5. Both the A6 and the A685 are bus service routes from Kendal, which is a useful help and avoids roadwalking. The ridge also lends itself well to the use of two cars by two parties walking the ridge in opposite directions and passing in the vicinity of Whinfell Beacon, the halfway point, each party returning in the other's car if they haven't forgotten to exchange car keys.

The ridgewalk is unsuitable for a wet or misty day, but a good alternative then is to walk down the length of Borrowdale from the gate on the A6 to Low Borrow Bridge — a delightful journey even in rain. There is only one occupied farm in the valley; another nearby is in ruins. Loneliness and loveliness go hand in hand here.

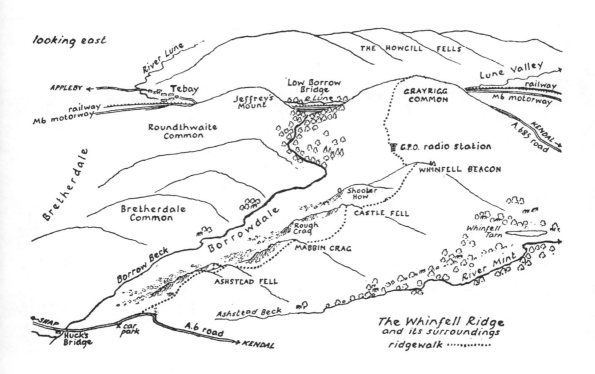

looking east

River Lune

THE HOWGILL FELLS

Lune Valley

APPLEBY ←

Tebay

Low Borrow Bridge

GRAYRIGG COMMON

railway

railway

Jeffrey's Mount

R. LUNE

M6 motorway

M6 motorway

Roundthwaite Common

A.685 road

KENDAL →

G.P.O. radio station

Bretherdale

WHINFELL BEACON

Bretherdale Common

Shooter How

Borrowdale

CASTLE FELL

Whinfell Tarn

Rough Crag

Borrow Beck

Mabbin Crag

River Mint

ASHSTEAD FELL

Ashstead Beck

SHAP

Huck's Bridge

car park

A.6 road

KENDAL →

The Whinfell Ridge
and its surroundings

ridgewalk ....

FROM THE A.6 ROAD NEAR HUCK'S BRIDGE

4 miles

There is a commodious parking area flanking the once busy and accident-prone (pre-motorway) Kendal-Shap road, A.6, between the site of the Leyland Clock and Huck's Bridge. From this, walk up the road to a gate recessed on the left and here gain access to the open fell. It is a steepish climb to the top of Ashstead Fell, which has three distinct summits. Beyond the third a low crosswall (no stile) is easily negotiated and the cairn on Mabbin Crag reached up a simple slope. Continue southeast to another crosswall and descend to the left alongside it to the Borrowdale valley, where Borrow Beck can be followed upstream to join a cart-track that leads to the gate on the A.6 used at the start of the walk.

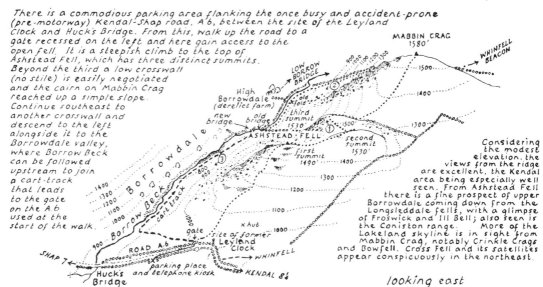

Considering the modest elevation, the views from the ridge are excellent, the Kendal area being especially well seen. From Ashstead Fell there is a fine prospect of upper Borrowdale coming down from the Longsleddale fells, with a glimpse of Froswick and Ill Bell; also seen is the Coniston range. More of the Lakeland skyline is in sight from Mabbin Crag, notably Crinkle Crags and Bowfell. Cross Fell and its satellites appear conspicuously in the northeast.

looking east

MAP

1
(2)

The threat to Borrowdale

With all the usual hamfistedness of bureaucracy, the Water Resources Board selected Conservation Year to threaten the drowning of more northern valleys. Among them, Borrowdale 'is deemed suitable for a reservoir'. It is probably hoped that there would be little opposition: after all, only a handful of folk make a living there, and although it is the most beautiful valley in Westmorland outside the Lake District this is not generally known and it has few visitors.

But do the water authorities really have to be so cannibalistic? *Must* they devour and destroy *for ever* areas of natural beauty that have taken ages to fashion? Must the sacrifice always be the homes of farmers, the pastures of animals, and plants and trees? Take the surplus water and be welcome to it, but can't it be done in a civilised way? Is it beyond the wit of their engineers to devise a scheme for taking water through underground pipes from inconspicuous intakes along the stream bed without the need and immense cost of constructing reservoirs? Well, is it?

Sooner or later the authorities will have to treat and use sea water. Why delay until more damage has been done to our heritage? Why don't they practice conservation as well as preach it? Lovely Borrowdale! Poor poor Borrowdale...

ONE MILE

SHAP

Huck's Bridge

parking place and telephone kiosk

BRETHERDALE

Borrowdale

ROAD A6

gate

cart track

KENDAL A6

gate

Borrow Beck

hut

900

1000

1100

1200

1300

Ashstead Fell

Combs Hollow

WHINFELL

1400

1500

900

800

barn

new bridge

site of former bridge

rain gauge

1000

1100

1200

1300

old fold

High Borrowdale (derelict farm)

MABBIN CRAG

1580

1500

1400

1300

1200

old fold

Low Borrowdale (farm)

Borrow Beck

800

WHINFELL BECK

The Leyland Clock

A roadside object familiar and friendly
to travellers along the A6 over Shap Fell
for almost fifty years has become (with
other popular establishments) a casualty
of this wellknown and notorious highway
following the opening of the alternative
route, M6, in October 1970.

The Leyland Clock, always so named, a
large double timepiece on a green pillar,
occupied a conspicuous site at the brow
of the hill descending to Huck's Bridge,
on the Kendal side.   Every passer-by
looked at it with affection even though
it did not always tell the correct time.
Many, from habit, will look for it still,
but it will help no more on the journey.

Castle Fell   Whinfell Beacon

The summit of Mabbin Crag

High Borrowdale —   once a farmhouse of distinction
in a beautiful situation.............
now a derelict ruin in a beautiful situation.

The top of Ashstead Fell

Although the name is applied generally to the
grassy summit above, Mabbin Crag is properly
the rocky eastern slope of the fell, this being
the roughest ground in the Borrowdale valley.
There are no cliffs here worth the attentions
of rockclimbers, but the tumbled boulders and scree
make the terrain difficult to negotiate. The descent
into Borrowdale from the summit should be made
only in the close company of one of the two walls
bounding the fell.
    The valley itself is interesting hereabouts,
Borrow Beck being a considerable stream
of translucent water adorned with
boulders of pink granite
washed down by floods.
The banks show distinct
flutings that suggest former
glacial activity. The picture
shows the abutments of the
former bridge, recently
replaced by a new one
100 yards upstream.
    A newly-installed
rain gauge nearby
implies an obvious
and familiar threat
to the valley.

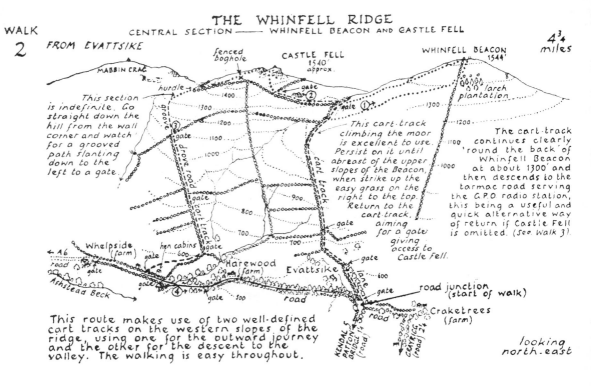

MAP

2
(2)

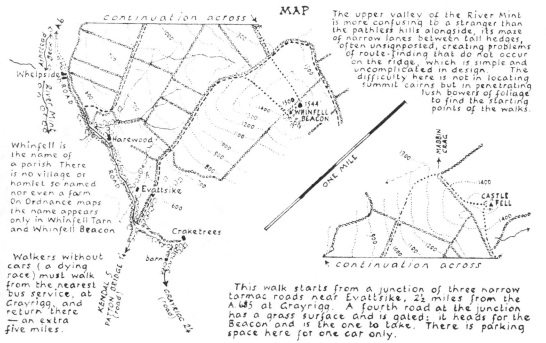

The upper valley of the River Mint
is more confusing to a stranger than
the pathless hills alongside, its maze
of narrow lanes between tall hedges,
often unsignposted, creating problems
of route-finding that do not occur
on the ridge, which is simple and
uncomplicated in design.   The
difficulty here is not in locating
summit cairns but in penetrating
lush bowers of foliage
to find the starting
points of the walks.

Whinfell is
the name of
a parish. There
is no village or
hamlet so named
nor even a farm.
On Ordnance maps
the name appears
only in Whinfell Tarn
and Whinfell Beacon.

Walkers without
cars (a dying
race) must walk
from the nearest
bus service, at
Grayrigg, and
return there
— an extra
five miles.

ONE MILE

This walk starts from a junction of three narrow
tarmac roads near Evattsike, 2½ miles from the
A.685 at Grayrigg. A fourth road at the junction
has a grass surface and is gated: it heads for the
Beacon and is the one to take. There is parking
space here for one car only.

*The summit of Castle Fell,
looking to Whinfell Beacon*

The plantation on Whinfell Beacon

A hundred feet lower than the summit of the Beacon,
on the southwest flank, there is a small plantation of
larch, a curious adornment in the midst of a
treeless expanse. Obviously put there by man,
its purpose is difficult to assess: it clearly
has no value as timber in so windswept
an environment and is not intended
as a shelter belt. The reason
lies in the use of the summit
as a beacon or signal station.
Here, on the site, always
available when needed,
is *firewood*.

The summit of
Whinfell Beacon

The view from Whinfell Beacon
The view is very extensive and
attractive to the south and west
but curtailed by higher fells to
the north and east.
Principal features:

The Kent Estuary 13	N Bretherdale Common 2
Flat Tarn 1	Cross Fell 24
Whinfell Tarn 1½	Little Dun Fell 23
SW Kendal 6	Great Dun Fell 22
Black Combe 29	NE Jeffrey's Mount 2
W The Coniston Fells 19	lower Borrowdale 1½
Crinkle Crags 20	The A.685 road at
Scafell 23	Low Borrow Bridge 2
Bowfell 21	The GPO radio
Great Gable 23	station ¾
Langdale Pikes 19	E Grayrigg Common 1½
High Raise 20	The Howgill Fells 3+
Ill Bell 10	Baugh Fell 11
Bannisdale 4	Rise Hill 12
Froswick 10	The Lune Valley 5
Thornthwaite Crag 11	Grayrigg Tarn 2
Helvellyn 17	SE Whernside 16
NW Harter Fell 9	Great Coum 13
upper Borrowdale 6	S The Bowland Fells 2?
Ashstead Fell 2	Farleton Knott 12
Mabbin Crag 1½	Benson Knott 4
Castle Fell ¾	Arnside Knott 16

Figures indicate distances in miles

FROM GRAYRIGG

6 miles, there and back by the same route.

This is the shortest and simplest way to the top of Whinfell Beacon from a bus stop. Except for the final half-mile it is all road-walking, but none the worse for that, the roads being quiet, traffic-free and very pleasant to stroll along.

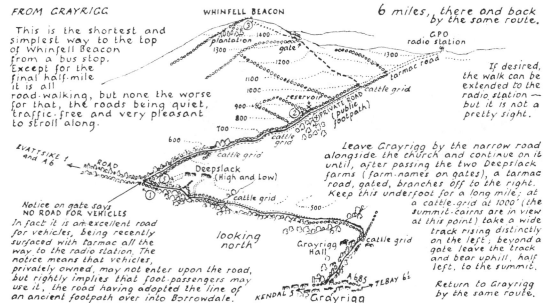

WHINFELL BEACON

GPO radio station

plantation
gate
reservoir
PRIVATE ROAD (public footpath)
cattle grid
cattle grid
tarmac road
cattle grid

1400
1300
1300
1200
1100
1000
900
800
700
600

EVATTSIKE 1 and A6 ←

ROAD

cattle grid

Deepslack
(High and Low)

cattle grid

500

looking
north

Grayrigg Hall

cattle grid

KENDAL 5   Grayrigg   TEBAY 6½

A685   TEBAY 6½

If desired, the walk can be extended to the radio station — but it is not a pretty sight.

Leave Grayrigg by the narrow road alongside the church and continue on it until, after passing the two Deepslack farms (farm-names on gates), a tarmac road, gated, branches off to the right. Keep this underfoot for a long mile; at a cattle-grid at 1000' (the summit-cairns are in view at this point) take a wide track rising distinctly on the left; beyond a gate leave the track and bear uphill, half left, to the summit.

Return to Grayrigg by the same route.

Notice on gate says
NO ROAD FOR VEHICLES

In fact it is an excellent road for vehicles, being recently surfaced with tarmac all the way to the radio station. The notice means that vehicles, privately owned, may not enter upon the road, but rightly implies that foot-passengers may use it, the road having adopted the line of an ancient footpath over into Borrowdale.

MAP

3
(2)

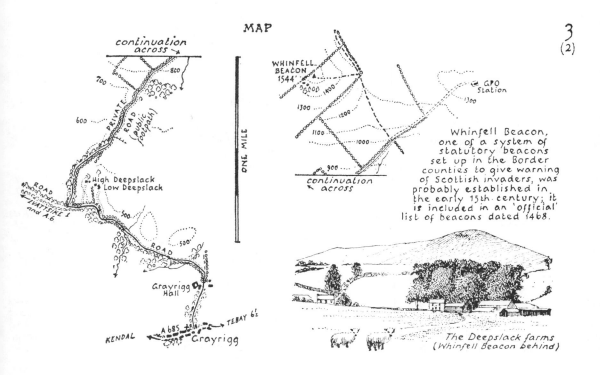

continuation
across →

800

700

600

PRIVATE ROAD (public footpath)

High Deepslack
Low Deepslack

ROAD

ROAD
KIRKBY
and A.6

500

500

Grayrigg
Hall

A 685
KENDAL   Grayrigg   TEBAY 6½

ONE MILE

WHINFELL
BEACON
1544

1500   1400

1300

1200

1100

1000

900

GPO
Station

1300

continuation
across →

Whinfell Beacon,
one of a system of
statutory beacons
set up in the Border
counties to give warning
of Scottish invaders, was
probably established in
the early 15th century; it
is included in an 'official'
list of beacons dated 1468.

The Deepslack farms
(Whinfell Beacon behind)

THE WHINFELL RIDGE
CENTRAL SECTION —— WHINFELL BEACON

6¼ miles

FROM BORROWDALE

The walk is deemed to start from the A.685
(bus service) at the entrance to Borrowdale,
which is recommended although cars
may be taken up the valley on tarmac
for ¾ mile and parked by a bridge
(marked P on diagram).
  Leave the valley-road 180 yards beyond
the second gate, where a cart-track
doubles back uphill on the left. Above
the treeline the path is less distinct
but can be followed to the ridge at
the radio station. Here incline right
over undulating ground, crossing a
wall to reach a good cart-track
encircling the summit of the Beacon,
which is gained by a simple climb.
Descend to the gate giving access to
Castle Fell and bear right along the
ridge of Shooter Howe, from which
go down (rough walking) to Borrow
Beck and rejoin the valley road,
returning along it to the A.685.

WHINFELL BEACON

C.P.O.
radio station

gate

CASTLE
FELL

1400

1300   1300   gate   1200

2   gate   1200

1100

line of path
indicated by
parapets→   1000   1200   1300

900   Shooter
Howe

800   4

good viewpoint

700   ←1100

←rough descent:
bracken, stones,
low crags.

900   800

Borrow Beck   looking
south

bridge   P   gate   P   Borrow Beck   farm road   Low Borrowdale
(farm)

KENDAL 9   Borrowdale
Wood   gate

A.685
railway   barn

NOWGILL 4

River Lune   →TEBAY 1

Low
Borrow Bridge   This is the best of the walks
in the Whinfell area, the approach
and return along Borrowdale being
delightful and the moorland section
rewarding in fine views.

MAP

4
(2)

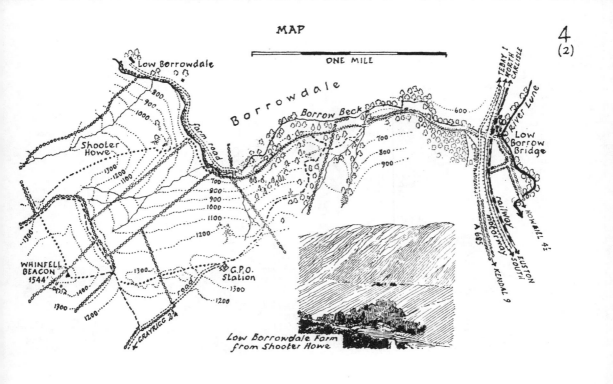

ONE MILE

Low Borrowdale

B o r r o w d a l e

Borrow Beck

Shooter Howe

farm road

800
900
1000

1300
1200
1100

700
800
900
1000
1100
1200

700

800

900

600

700

WHINFELL
BEACON
1544'

1300
1400

1300

1200

G.P.O.
Station

road

1300

1200

TEBAY 1
NORTH
CARLISLE

River Lune

Low
Borrow
Bridge

railway

motorway

KENDAL 9

A 685

HOWGILL 4½

EUSTON
SOUTH

CRAYRIGG 2¼

Low Borrowdale Farm
from Shooter Howe

4
(3)

Whinfell Beacon:
20th century version.

In the picture
the two simple
cairns marking
the 15th century
signal station
appear below
the platform
of the 20th
century ditto,
illustrating
what is
jocularly
known as
technical
progress.

When this apparition bursts upon the
vision at close range, one's instinct is
to flee the place, screaming. But the
contraption is NOT a nuclear missile or
a spaceship from Mars. It is a G.P.O.
radio repeater station, unmanned, used
for boosting messages over the hills. It
first appeared on the Whinfell skyline
unheralded and unsung, a few years ago.
One can applaud fervently the desire to
restore 1840 standards to postal services,
but what a price to have to pay! A
monstrosity like this should never have
been allowed to disgrace Whinfell. Was
planning permission necessary? Was it
sought? Was it granted? Or can a
national authority do as it pleases with
the nation's landscape?

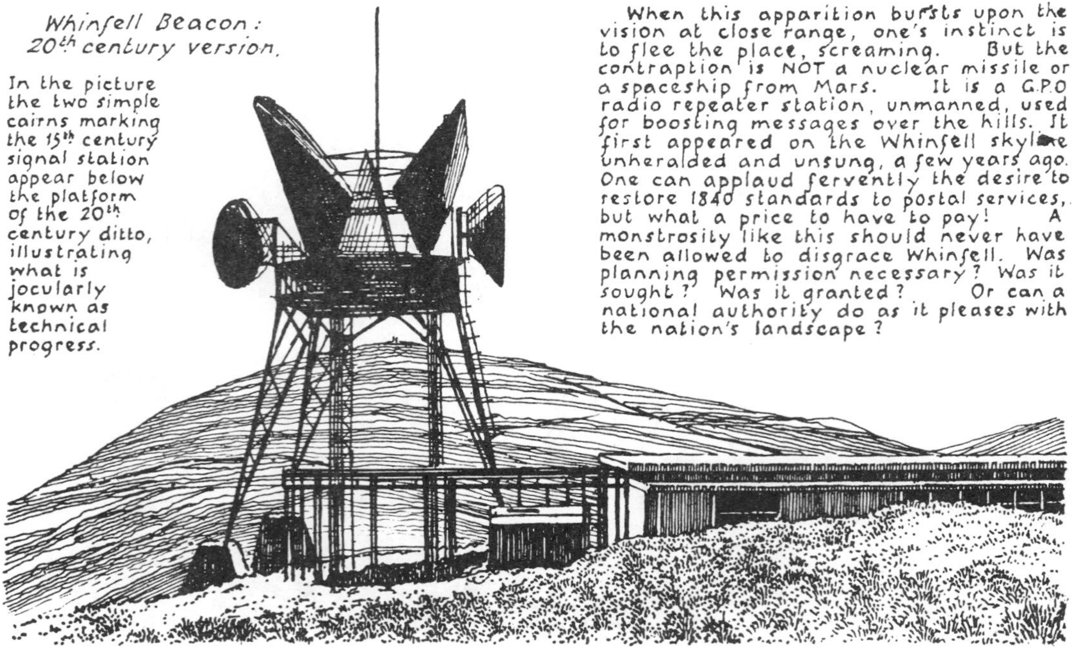

A bathing pool, Borrow Beck

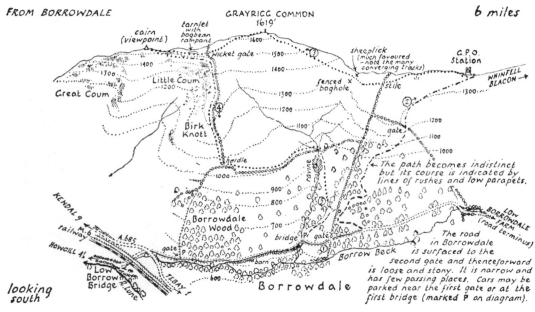

MAP

5
(2)

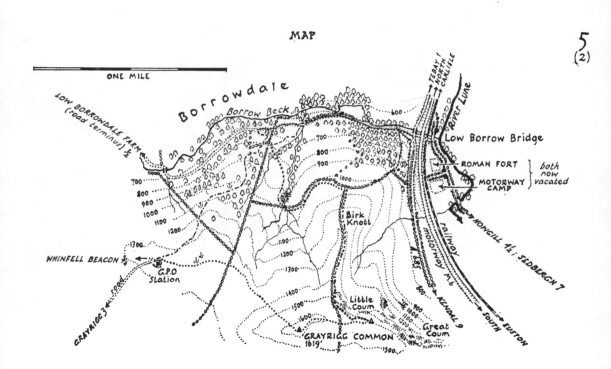

ONE MILE

Borrowdale

Borrow Beck

LOW BORROWDALE FARM
(road terminus)

TEBAY
NORTH CARLILE

River Lune

Low Borrow Bridge

ROMAN FORT
MOTORWAY CAMP
} both now vacated

600

700

800

900

1000

700
800
900
1000
1100
1200

Birk Knott

1100

1300

WHINFELL BEACON

G.P.O Station

1200

1300

HOWGILL 4½ : SEDBERGH 7

railway

motorway M6

KENDAL 9

SOUTH EUSTON

GRAYRIGG 3 — road

1400

1500

1600

Little Coum

Great Coum

800
900
1000
1100
1200

GRAYRIGG COMMON
1619'

1500

The walk starts from the Kendal-Appleby road (bus service) at the entrance to the Borrowdale valley. Go along the road into Borrowdale for a mile. 180 yards beyond the second gate take a rough cart-track, on the left, up the wooded hillside. Above the treeline the path, now indistinct, passes through a gate in a cross-wall to reach the ridge at the G.P.O station. Now turn left along the pathless ridge, using a stile in the next wall to gain access to the grassy slope rising to the Ordnance column on the top of Grayrigg Common. A detour to the cairn overlooking Great and Little Coums is recommended for its aerial view: reach it by continuing eastwards and using a wicket-gate in an intervening wall. Return by descending alongside the wall over Birk Knott to a T-junction of walls. The starting-point may be regained by an unauthorised beeline down the slope, but respecters of trespass, as readers are assumed to be, will use the hurdle in the corner and take a circuitous and pleasanter course by following the wall running west until it is breached by a gap where a low fence spans a tributary beck (note that this gap may alternatively be reached directly from the Ordnance column).

Cross the wall here and descend by a fine ravine to the valley road across a damp pasture notable for its wealth of summer flowers. Join the road at a bridge and return along it to the A. 685.

Purple Orchid

Bird's Eye Primrose

The road in Barrowdale

← MAP OF THE ROUTE OVERLEAF

The summit of Grayrigg Common

The Howgill Fells

The cairn above the Coums

From this vantage point the prospect of the Lune Gorge, with its multiplicity of new lines of communication, is excellent.

Tebay

motorway

The Ordnance column (S.5663) on the top of Grayrigg Common marks the greatest elevation on the Whinfell ridge and the panorama is very extensive. Most of the Lakeland skyline is in view, with the Scafells and Great Gable prominent above Whinfell Beacon. Cross Fell and its satellites are visible northwards. Nearby the Howgill Fells hide much of the Pennines; Whernside, however, can be seen above the charming Lunesdale and Dentdale valleys. The Bowland hills appear southwards and the district of the Kent Estuary, beyond Kendal, completes the view. The new motorway, north from Killington Reservoir to the high ground near Shap, is a new and conspicuous feature in the landscape.

Great Coum

Little Coum

Low Borrow Bridge

The Romans were the first to note the attractions of the little delta in the Lune Gorge where Borrow Beck joins the main river, and they stationed a garrison here. Little is now to be seen of the earthworks of this fort but its existence has been confirmed by excavations on the site. Many interesting discoveries are displayed in Kendal Museum.

After the departure of the Romans the area reverted to its former wild inhospitability, a place without habitations. A thousand years passed by with only the occasional nomadic visitor before the gradual cultivation of the land by native settlers and the establishing of a few farms brought a change to the scene. A rough road linking Kendal and Appleby developed from the tracks of early travellers and threaded an uneasy course through the hills. But Low Borrow Bridge remained quiet.

The construction of the main-line railway last century caused a temporary disturbance in the life of the valley but even the thundering expresses did little to alter its character.

Recent changes in travelling habits, with emphasis on wider and faster carriageways for increased road traffic, have, however, altered Low Borrow Bridge out of all recognition in the past few years. What was peaceful has become turbulent. What was rural has become urban. The sounds of the countryside are drowned by the noise of commerce.

The Kendal-Appleby road, A.685, has been re-routed (as have the Howgill and Borrowdale junctions); hitherto a narrow and tortuous lane, it has become a fast highway. The new Motorway, M.6, runs alongside this local road, between it and the railway. The temporary camp of the army of workers occupied a field next to the Roman fort and once more the place was a hive of intense activity.

Low Borrow Bridge will never be the same again. But it keeps its name, in the singular, although there is now a plurality of bridges, all crossing Borrow Beck — a new bridge for local traffic and a mammoth span for the M.6, both of concrete and contrasting sharply with the stone railway viaduct, a structure of Victorian solidity. The original Low Borrow Bridge is quite insignificant in the new scheme of things and virtually obsolete. The area may acquire fresh fame as a rock-climbing ground, a mile of cliffs having been left naked by blasting.

The Romans left no scars in the valley. The Motorwaymen have left plenty.

19th century......

.........20th century

PART TWO
THE HOWGILL FELLS

THE HOWGILL FELLS

INTRODUCTION

In the midst of the undulating rural terrain between the Lake District and the Yorkshire Dales there rises abruptly a compact cluster of hills some forty square miles in extent, very clearly defined by encircling valleys. This group is commonly known as the Howgill Fells (rather curiously taking the name of a tiny hamlet along its western base in preference to that of the town of Sedbergh at the southern extremity) but the cartographers of the Ordnance Survey have never identified the group by a single name, using on their maps only the local names for undefined grazing areas. It is understood, however, that the intention of the Ordnance Survey is to adopt, in future editions of their maps, the name "Howgill Fells" for the whole mass of high ground.

In appearance the Howgill Fells are quite unlike the craggy mountains of Lakeland to the west or the rolling Yorkshire moors to the east: they are particularly distinctive. They are sleek and smooth, looking, from a distance, like velvet curtains in sunlight, like silken drapes at sunset; they are steep-sided but gently domed, and beautiful in a way that few hilly areas are. Their soaring and sweeping lines are not interrupted by walls or fences above the intakes, giving a splendid upland expanse of 'free range' walking. As in Lakeland, access to the hills is unrestricted and there are no trespass notices and no prohibited shooting areas — just wander where you wish, but of course with a sense of responsibility and respect for the rights and property of the farmers. The compactness of the group is emphasised by a remarkable concentration of summits, often likened to a huddle of squatting elephants, there being a score of different and distinct tops around 2000 feet in the central area, which is properly an

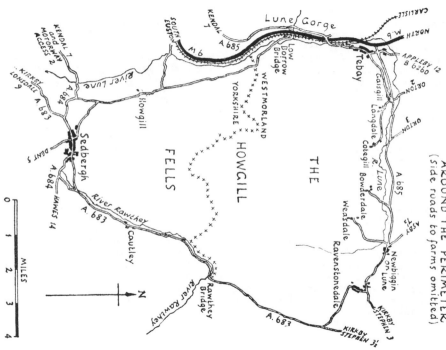

THE HOWGILL FELLS —

ACCESS ROADS AROUND THE PERIMETER
(side roads to farms omitted)

Legend:

━━━━ Motorway M6
━━━ Other roads
✚✚✚✚ Railway
✕✕✕✕✕ County boundary

Note that it is planned to re-route the A685 road between Gaisgill and Newbiggin on the track of the former railway

There are two convenient access points on the Motorway — one at Killington (where the Kendal–Sedbergh road crosses) and the other north of Tebay

0 ½ 1 2 3 4
MILES

N

THE HOWGILL FELLS

Lune Gorge
CARLISLE
NORTH M6
APPLEBY 12 B6260
TEBAY
Gaisgill
Langdale
Orton 2
Orton 5
SOUTH EUSTON
KENDAL 7
A685
Low Borrow Bridge
M6
River Lune
WESTMORLAND
YORKSHIRE
Howgill
KIRKBY LONSDALE 9
KENDAL 7 and MOTORWAY ACCESS 2
A684
A683
Sedbergh
DENT 5
A684
HAWES 14
Cautley
River Rawthey
A683
Rawthey Bridge
River Rawthey
A683
KIRKBY STEPHEN 7½
KIRKBY STEPHEN 3½
Newbiggin on Lune
ASH 7½
Cotegill
Bowderdale
Weasdale
Ravenstonedale
R. Lune
THE
HOWGILL
FELLS

undulating plateau from which ridges radiate like the spokes of a wheel, enclosing deep valleys that run to all points of the compass but have a common objective —— all their streams are feeders of the River Lune. The Howgill Fells are wholly within the Lune catchment area and therefore west of the main Pennine watershed. They are crossed by the boundary between Westmorland and Yorkshire, the former county claiming most of the area and the smaller section in Yorkshire being a part of the Dales National Park.

Outside the immediate district the Howgill Fells are not widely known. They are remote from large centres of population and the usual routes of travel across the Pennines. There is car access to the perimeter on every side but mostly on quiet minor roads used only by local traffic. The main railway line to Scotland skirts the north-western corner on its journey up the spectacular Lune Gorge, where the hills appear suddenly with startling effect, and many travellers must have admired them fleetingly from the train windows. But the recent completion of the Motorway M6, which on this section accompanies the railway and gives even more dramatic views of the western facade of the Howgills, will bring them to the notice of far more people and earn for them the attention they so well deserve. An age of obscurity and neglect is over.

The heights in the south are well enough known to Sedbergh folk and to the boys of Sedbergh School particularly, but otherwise are visited only by a few discerning walkers who appreciate their quietness and seclusion. But elsewhere in the group it is unusual indeed to meet anyone other than an occasional shepherd: in fact the meeting of Stanley and Dr. Livingstone could hardly have been more poignant than the confrontation of one walker by another in the northern sector —— it simply does not happen.   One can walk all day here knowing full well that not another soul will be seen, and

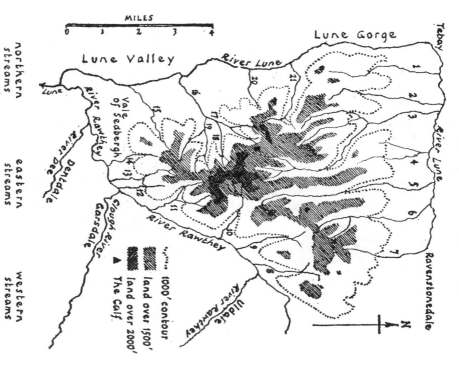

THE HOWGILL FELLS — PHYSICAL FEATURES

MILES
0 1 2 3 4

Lune Gorge

Lune Valley

River Lune

Tebay

Ravenstonedale

Vale of Sedbergh

River Rawthey

River Dee

Dentdale

Garsdale

Clough River

River Rawthey

Uldale

The Calf

.... 1000' contour
land over 1500'
land over 2000'
▲ The Calf

N

northern streams

1: Tebaygill Beck
2: Ellergill Beck
3: Langdale Beck
4: Cotegill Beck
5: Bowderdale Beck
6: Weasdale Beck
7: Dale Gill (source of the Lune)

eastern streams

8: Wandale Beck
9: Backside Beck (Westerdale)
10: Cautley Holme Beck
11: Hobdale Beck
12: Little Ashbeck
13: Ashbeck Gill
14: Settlebeck Gill

western streams

15: Crosedale Beck
16: Chapel Beck
17: Long Rigg Beck
18: Calf Beck
19: Bram Rigg Beck
20: Fairmile Beck
21: Carlingill Beck

Northern and western streams are direct feeders of the Lune.
Eastern streams flow first into the Rawthey, a tributary

that one's footsteps may never again be trodden for years. It is the utter loneliness of the surroundings that constitutes the one (and only) hazard for the solitary walker, not the menace of crags or rough ground. In fact conditions underfoot are everywhere delightfully easy and objective dangers are absent. But a companion is advised — just in case. Sheep are no help in the event of accident or illness. In mist the wilder places should really be left alone. The central mass of high ground can be confusing, even in clear weather, because of the similarity of the various summits and an absence of distinguishing features, while the descending ridges conform to a common pattern, so that without constant reference to the map it is easy to wander hopelessly off course; further, mistakes of navigation cannot be rectified without retracing steps, the dividing upland valleys being much too eroded and steep-sided to be crossed by bee-lines. The seven ridges running down to the north especially are bewilderingly alike, each a twin to the next, all descending gradually and lacking landmarks until the intakes and valley farmsteads are reached. Incidentally, it is sad to see so many abandoned and ruinous farmhouses and barns around the Howgills. Times were better here in the old days.

Public footpaths and bridleways are few, but there are good drove roads (used for bringing down the sheep) on all the fells, and the pedestrian on the unfrequented northern heights is considerably aided in his progress and in his route-finding by the imprint of tractors in the grass. Farmers never seem to walk where they can ride, nowadays, even when doing their rounds of the tops to check their sheep; consequently all the long northern ridges carry distinct tractor tracks that lead down unerringly to the valley farms. Cairns are a luxury rarely seen in the Howgills. Walkers' routes have no guidance of this sort but some of the summits have cairns, usually small because stones are at a premium on the grassy tops.

The basic rocks of the hills belong to the Silurian period and are mainly a durable grey sandstone of the type known as Coniston Grit, widely used in local building but not greatly in evidence *in situ*, rarely outcropping and being extensive on the surface only at Cautley Crag and Black Force. There are no attractions for rock-climbers. In the extreme north-east corner, at Ravenstonedale, is a bed of carboniferous limestone with all its attendant scenic delights — but no subterranean passages or potholes for the caver to explore. The Howgill Fells are exclusively for the fellwalker pure and simple — if such there be... The effect of glacial action is seen in the smooth slopes and rounded summits, suggesting that the whole area must have been covered in ages past by a massive ice-cap.

Botanically the district is rich, displaying a more diverse and interesting flora than Lakeland, perhaps because of its isolation and comparative lack of footpaths. It is the deeply eroded ravines and side valleys that shelter most species, the upper slopes being well clothed in grasses and mosses but bare of flowers. Heather occurs only sparsely. Bracken is rampant.

The place-names have a close affinity with those of the Lake District. Here, too, streams are becks, ravines are gills, valleys are dales, hills are fells and clearings are thwaites. Here, in or around the Howgills, is another Langdale, another Borrowdale, another Bowderdale, another Grisedale. And another Harter Fell.

Before the Norsemen settled here, the Romans established a fortified camp at Low Borrow Bridge with roads therefrom to north and south, and earlier civilisations have left their traces in the valleys. But the high ground has no historical associations. One old track across the tops is still referred to as Scot Rake, but appears to have had no significance except as a drove road. Man has never regarded these hills as a home or as a place of refuge. They have always been lonely.

Mention must be made of the creatures on the heights. Buzzards are often seen wheeling in the sky, and kestrels and ravens and crows also nest high above the valleys, while the lower pastures are especially rich in bird life. Foxes and hares roam the hills, ever alert for the arch-enemy man, but the peculiar joy of the Howgills is the fell ponies, which wander as they fancy: delightful creatures with flowing manes and tails, usually brown in colour but often piebald. Their growing numbers are viewed with apprehension by the farmers, for they graze on the sweetest grass, which sheep also favour — and the sheep are the farmers' living. Incidentally, the sheep on the Howgills are very handsome specimens: the black-faced, white-fleeced Rough Fell; it is an endearing habit of theirs to regard a passing walker almost with disbelief — which is not at all surprising.

In one respect — in the magnificence of the views — the Howgills win first prize. Here you have the best of all worlds: uninterrupted views of Lakeland's fine mountains; a glittering seascape; fifty miles of the Pennine skyline; a vista of the limestone peaks of Yorkshire. From the highest point, The Calf, the distant scene is unexcelled. There is not a more extensive panorama in England than this. And all that is seen is fair to look upon.

Sedbergh (pronounced *Sedber*), a small market town catering for the large Public School long established in its midst, is the 'capital' of the region and the only community of any size around the perimeter. There is a fair amount of good accommodation here and two caravan sites nearby. Ravenstonedale and Tebay, in the other corners of the Howgill triangle, both have hotels and cottage accommodation. At Cautley there is a popular inn. A few scattered farmhouses offer bed and breakfast, but in general the farmers are concerned with farming, not with catering: this is not, as yet, a recognized holiday or tourist centre. If a car is available, Kendal is a good base, all parts of the district being within an hour's journey.

Infrequent buses serve the district, but not with any primary intention of catering for walkers, and there are no local train services. A visitor who is not staying overnight really needs a car to reach and explore the area, and the walks described in this book have been designed accordingly, to start and finish at the same point (where a car can be parked), although in almost all cases alternative ways of return are given to avoid going over the same ground twice. A walker independent of a car can enjoy excellent cross-country expeditions by linking routes together but should be sure of his bed for the night. The ideal arrangement is for two parties, each with a car, to do 'through' walks from different starting places, passing en route to swap car keys.

As more and more people flee to the countryside for a brief respite from the towns, the opportunities of quiet rural enjoyment are shrinking. The heavy weekend traffic to Lakeland and the Dales, for instance, destroys the peace that people come to seek. As yet the Howgills are relatively unknown. They are not, and never will be, a popular magnet, and in this lack of general appeal lies their great attraction for those who want to escape from the noise and the crowds. Here is a pervading tranquillity.

It remains to be seen whether the Motorway will bring a new prosperity to the area. This is lovely country, but it is stagnating and needs infusing with new interests appropriate to its character. Economic pressures have ousted many of the small farmers and the closing of the railways and a curtailment of bus services has caused deprivation, especially at Tebay. The Howgills are too proud, and yet too modest, to advertise themselves, but publicity could do much to arouse a greater awareness of their charms and assist the development of the area on new lines: catering for tourists and visitors. Sedbergh publishes an excellent guidebook, informative and authoritative and exceptionally well written, but more could be done. The

Howgills want putting on the map: they have what many people increasingly seek. What is needed is _not_ a plan for fancy hotels and amusement parks and chairlifts and motor scrambles, heaven forbid, nor large-scale forests and reservoirs — for such innovations would rob the district of the unique character that makes it so distinctive and in which lies its salvation — nor even the sighting of a monster in the Lune or a dinosaur in Bowderdale. It is not a plan that is needed, nor changes in the landscape, nor a sensational attraction to bring coachloads of rubbernecks, but a steady influx of quiet orderly visitors who enjoy hill-country as nature fashioned it. The Howgills would be superb territory for pony-trekking, and they look (to a non-skier!) ideal for winter expeditions, but their greatest appeal must ever be to those who love to walk freely 'over the tops' and commune with nature in solitude. There is no better place for doing this than the Howgill Fells, bless them.

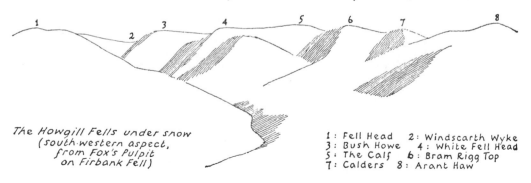

The Howgill Fells under snow
(south-western aspect,
from Fox's Pulpit
on Firbank Fell)

1: Fell Head   2: Windscarth Wyke
3: Bush Howe   4: White Fell Head
5: The Calf   6: Bram Rigg Top
7: Calders   8: Arant Haw

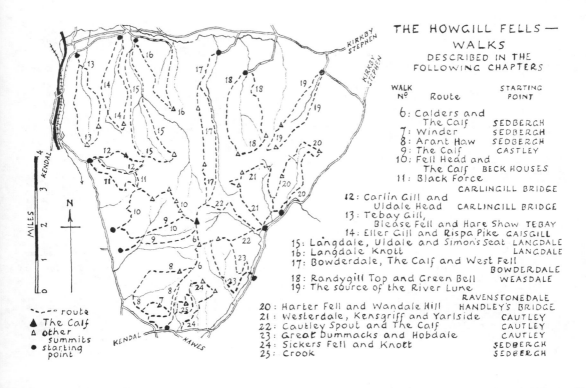

THE HOWGILL FELLS —
WALKS
DESCRIBED IN THE FOLLOWING CHAPTERS

MILES
4
3
2
1
0

KENDAL

N

KIRKBY STEPHEN

---- route
▲ The Calf
△ other summits
● starting point

KENDAL   HAWES

This is the classic high-level walk on the
Howgill Fells: a favourite excursion and
the only one generally well known. It
traverses the highest ground, passes
through typical scenery, has superb
views and serves as an excellent
introduction to the group.

There are two ways out of Sedbergh to the
open fell: (A) from Howgill Lane to the
path rising across the breast
of Winder; (B) alongside
Settlebeck Gill.
Preferably,
go by B and
return by A.

THE CALF 2220'

Cautley
Crag

Bram Rigg
Top
CALDERS

GREAT
DUMMACKS

ARANT HAW
1989'

old
fold x

Hobdale Beck

Middle Tongue

WINDER
1551'

Crosedale Beck

CROOK

Ashbeck Gill

Settlebeck Gill

The wire fence
around the head of Hobdale
is the only exception to the
rule that there are no walls
or fences on the higher parts
of the Howgill Fells.

A   B

gate   gate   waterfall

farm   barn   reservoir gates

Sedbergh

HOWGILL   car park

KENDAL
10
Church

KIRKBY STEPHEN 14
HAWES 15

Hill
(farm)

From the main street turn up Joss Lane (between
the Congregational Church and a public car park) to its
end at a gate with Hill Farm ahead. Incline left across
a field to a pleasant wooded dell and ascend it, using stiles,
to a kissing gate in the intake wall. Take the path rising to
the left and proceed above the west bank of Settlebeck Gill; when
the path fades, a line of rushes indicates the route. The main path
from Sedbergh is joined at 1600' and the way forward is clear. Arant
Haw is skirted and a steep climb follows by a fence to the top of Calders.
From the cairn aim north, leaving the fence. The path is indistinct here
but improves on Bram Rigg Top, where it descends to a col, beyond which
an easy climb on grass leads to the summit of The Calf.

So direct and well-defined is this route that there is not really a
better alternative way back to Sedbergh, but it is no deprivation to
tread the same ground twice in this case, the views in descent being
excellent. Detours may, however, be easily made to the tops of Arant Haw
and Winder before descending to the town by the path down to Howgill Lane(A).

looking northwest

MAP

6
(2)

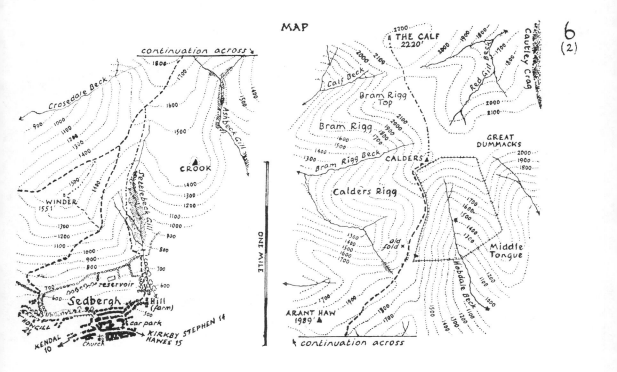

continuation across

Crosdale Beck

1600
1700
1600
1500
1500
1400

Ashbeck Gill

900 1000 1100 1200 1300 1400

1500
1400

1300
1200
1100

CROOK ▲

WINDER
1551

1300
1200
1100
1000
900
800

Settlebeck Gill

900
800
700
600

reservoir

700
800

500

Sedbergh

Hill (farm)

500

600

NONGILL

KENDAL 10   Church   KIRKBY STEPHEN 14
HAWES 15

car park

ONE MILE

THE CALF 2220'
2200
2100
2000
1900 1800 1800 1700

Calf Beck

Bram Rigg Top

Bram Rigg

Cautley Crag
1300

Red Gill Beck

2000
2100

GREAT DUMMACKS
2000
1900
1800

2100
1900 1800 1700
1600
1500
1400
1300

Bram Rigg Beck   CALDERS

Calders Rigg

1700
1600
1500
1400
1300

Middle Tongue

1300
1200
1100
1000

1300 1400 1500 1600 1700

old fold ×

Hobdale Beck

1500
1400
1300
1200

1700
1800

1700   1800

ARANT HAW
1989' ▲

1800
1100
1400

continuation across

Three sections of the walk

Winder to Arant Haw

Arant Haw to Calders

Calders to Bram Rigg Top and The Calf

Bram Rigg Top   THE CALF

The altitude of Calders

It is commonly assumed that the highest point on the Howgill Fells is occupied by the Ordnance Survey column on The Calf, at 2220' (amended to 2219' recently), and this is almost certainly true. However, other undulations of the plateau have not as yet been measured exactly. There are two other 2200' contour rings, at Bram Rigg Top and at Calders, but none of 2225'.

Bram Rigg Top is clearly the lowest of the three — it is overtopped by Calders when viewed from The Calf, and by The Calf when seen from Calders — and can therefore be dismissed as a contender for the honour.

Not so Calders. The 2200' contour is here much less extensive than that on The Calf but Calders is the more peaked, the ground within the contour rising more quickly above the contour line. The altitude of Calders has not been determined by instruments, unfortunately, and the accuracy of the contour cannot be completely relied upon.

As it happens, the cairn on Calders, when seen from The Calf, appears alongside the outline of Ingleborough (2373'), the top 200' or so of which is visible. This suggests that the summit of The Calf must be slightly higher than that of Calders, the view to the latter being imperceptibly *down*. Of course Ingleborough is 15 miles distant and not in the same horizontal plane, but the curvature of the earth can't curve all that much in 15 miles.

My guess is that Calders is 2215'.

The summit of The Calf

O.S. column
No S 5676

Large-scale Ordnance maps indicate a 'Standing Stone' 400 yards northeast of the column. It should be easy to spot, stones of any sort being a rarity here in the universal grassiness, but it is found only by diligent search, no longer standing but reclining and of lesser proportions than expected. A benchmark is cut into it.

INGLEBOROUGH

looking from The Calf to Calders

2220'
CALF

CALDERS

horizontal line

2373'

line of vision, slightly downward →

2173'

∴ Calders is lower than The Calf.   Q.E.D.

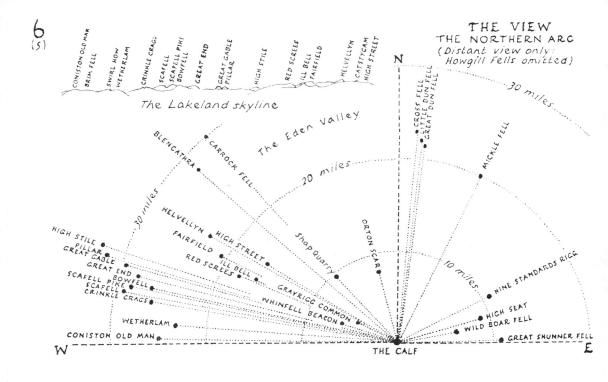

THE VIEW
THE NORTHERN ARC
(Distant view only: Howgill Fells omitted)

The Lakeland skyline

CONISTON OLD MAN, BRIM FELL, SWIRL HOW, WETHERLAM, CRINKLE CRAGS, SCAFELL, SCAFELL PIKE, BOWFELL, GREAT END, GREAT GABLE, PILLAR, HIGH STILE, RED SCREES, ILL BELL, FAIRFIELD, HELVELLYN, CATSTYCAM, HIGH STREET

The Eden Valley

CROSS FELL, LITTLE DUN FELL, GREAT DUN FELL

30 miles

BLENCATHRA, CARROCK FELL

MICKLE FELL

20 miles

HELVELLYN, HIGH STREET

FAIRFIELD, ILL BELL

RED SCREES

SHAP QUARRY

ORTON SCAR

HIGH STILE, PILLAR, GREAT GABLE

10 miles

NINE STANDARDS RIGG

GREAT END, BOWFELL

SCAFELL PIKE, SCAFELL, CRINKLE CRAGS

GRAYRIGG COMMON

WHINFELL BEACON

HIGH SEAT, WILD BOAR FELL

WETHERLAM

CONISTON OLD MAN

W   THE CALF   E

GREAT SHUNNER FELL

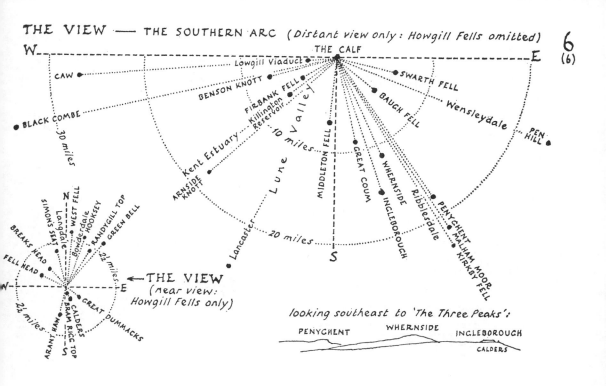

THE VIEW — THE SOUTHERN ARC (Distant view only: Howgill Fells omitted)

6
(6)

W ———————— THE CALF ———————— E

Lowgill Viaduct
CAW
SWARTH FELL
BENSON KNOTT
BAUGH FELL
FIRBANK FELL
Wensleydale
BLACK COMBE
Killington Reservoir
30 miles
PEN HILL
Kent Estuary
10 miles
MIDDLETON FELL
ARNSIDE KNOTT
GREAT COUM
Lune Valley
WHERNSIDE
INGLEBOROUGH
Ribblesdale
PENYGHENT
MALHAM MOOR
KIRKBY FELL
Lancaster
20 miles
S

N
WEST FELL
SIMON'S SEAT
Langdale
Bowderdale
HOOKSEY
RANDYGILL TOP
GREEN BELL
BREAKS HEAD
2½ miles
FELL HEAD
W ——————— E
THE VIEW
(near view: Howgill Fells only)
CALDERS
GREAT DUMMACKS
2½ miles
BRAM RIGG TOP
ARANT HAW
2½ miles
S

looking southeast to 'The Three Peaks':

PENYGHENT   WHERNSIDE   INGLEBOROUGH
CALDERS

'Winder' is pronounced prosaically,
not poetically, with a short 'i' —— as
Eliza Doolittle would have pronounced
'window' pre-Higgins.

It might create a wrong impression to say that
Winder is to Sedbergh what the Matterhorn is
to Zermatt, but the relationship is the same.
The hill and the town are very closely linked.
Winder dominates Sedbergh and its valley.
Signposts in the town that point the way
'TO THE FELL' really mean 'TO WINDER'.
Everybody in Sedbergh knows
Winder, none more thoroughly
(for a brief but memorable
episode in their careers)
than the boys of the
School, whose
playground and
training ground it is
and whose memories of
it remain through life;
indeed, the school song
is called 'Winder': "It is
Cautley, Calf and Winder
that makes the Sedbergh man."
Winder is steep, but benign and
friendly. It is easy to climb and
commands a glorious panorama of
the peaks of Lakeland, the mid-Lune
valley and Morecambe Bay, while the
terrace-walk across its breast is a most
delightful promenade overlooking the town
and the lovely valleys of Garsdale and Dentdale.
Many a non-Sedberghian has a
high regard for Winder, too........

looking north

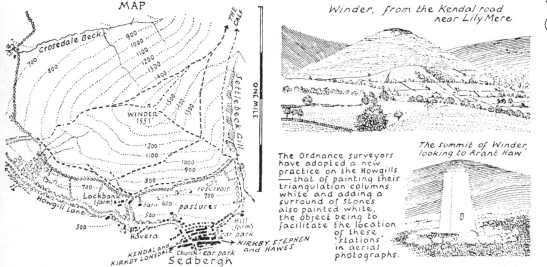

MAP

Crosedale Beck

THE CALF

900
1000
1100
1200
1300
1400
1500

WINDER 1551

Settlebeck Gill

ONE MILE

1400
1300
1200
1100
1000
900
800
700

600
700

reservoir
700

Lockbank (farm)

farm 600

pastures

500

500

Havera

Hill (farm) car park

KENDAL and
KIRKBY LONSDALE

KIRKBY STEPHEN
and HAWES

Church car park

HOWGILL Howgill Lane

700
800

Sedbergh

Winder, from the Kendal road near Lily Mere

The Ordnance surveyors have adopted a new practice on the Howgills — that of painting their triangulation columns white and adding a surround of stones also painted white, the object being to facilitate the location of these 'stations' in aerial photographs.

The summit of Winder, looking to Arant Haw.

Winder has a 'moat' of private pastures, but there are two ways through to the fell from the town:
A: via Howgill Lane (which leaves the main street at the Golden Lion) and Lockbank Farm; and
B: via Joss Lane (which leaves the main street at the Congregational Church) and Hill Farm.
Preferably use A both going and returning, saving B for the ascent of The Calf.
Above the intake wall, do the walk clockwise, following the arrowed route on the diagram.
Enterprising pedestrians have created other paths; to avoid confusion only regular routes are shown.

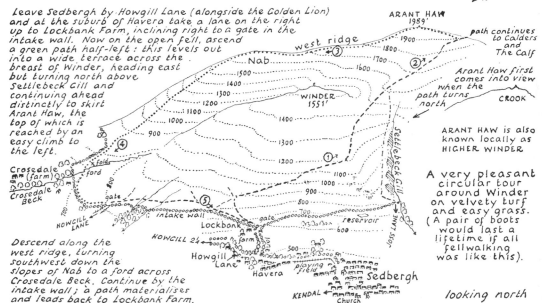

Leave Sedbergh by Howgill Lane (alongside the Golden Lion) and at the suburb of Havera take a lane on the right up to Lockbank Farm, inclining right to a gate in the intake wall. Now on the open fell, ascend a green path half-left: this levels out into a wide terrace across the breast of Winder, heading east but turning north above Settlebeck Gill and continuing ahead distinctly to skirt Arant Haw, the top of which is reached by an easy climb to the left.

ARANT HAW
1989'

path continues to Calders and The Calf

west ridge

Nab

WINDER
1551'

CROOK

Arant Haw first comes into view when the path turns north

ARANT HAW is also known locally as HIGHER WINDER

Settlebeck Gill

A very pleasant circular tour around Winder on velvety turf and easy grass. (A pair of boots would last a lifetime if all fellwalking was like this).

Crosedale (farm)
Crosedale Beck

fold
ford

gate
intake wall

Lockbank farm

HOWGILL LANE

HOWGILL 2¼

Howgill Lane

Havera

reservoir

JOSS LANE

playing field

Sedbergh

KENDAL
Church

Descend along the west ridge, turning southwest down the slopes of Nab to a ford across Crosedale Beck. Continue by the intake wall; a path materialises and leads back to Lockbank Farm.

looking north

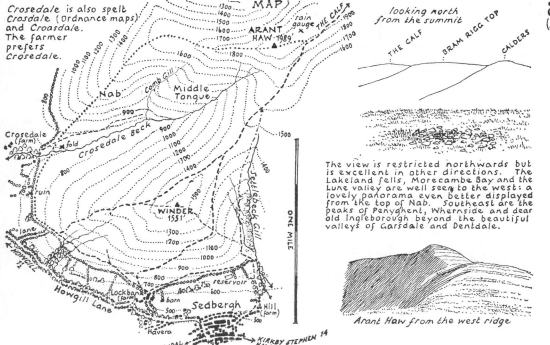

Crosedale is also spelt *Crosdale* (Ordnance maps) and *Croasdale*. The farmer prefers *Crosedale*.

MAP

rain gauge

ARANT HAW 1989 ▲

THE CALF

Nab

Comb Gill

Middle Tongue

Crosedale (farm)

fold

Crosedale Beck

ruin

lane

▲ WINDER 1551

Settlebeck Gill

ONE MILE

KNOTT

Howgill Lane

Lockbank (farm)

barn

reservoir

Hill (farm)

Sedbergh

Haverah

KENDAL 10   Church   KIRKBY STEPHEN 14
HAWES 15

looking north from the summit

THE CALF   BRAM RIGG TOP   CALDERS

The view is restricted northwards but is excellent in other directions. The Lakeland fells, Morecambe Bay and the Lune valley are well seen to the west: a lovely panorama even better displayed from the top of Nab. Southeast are the peaks of Penyghent, Whernside and dear old Ingleborough beyond the beautiful valleys of Garsdale and Dentdale.

Arant Haw from the west ridge

One feels really amongst the hills, intimately so, on this impressive expedition. This is a beautiful walk, with the advantage (rare in the Howgills) of distinct paths almost all the way.

Miles on this diagram are measured from Four Lane Ends, not Castley Farm.

Parking a car at Four Lane Ends is a problem. It is possible to squeeze a small one against the hedge, but there is more space 150 yards down the road going west (signposted 'Lowgill')

FELL HEAD   Breaks Head   Bush Howe   White Fell Head   THE CALF

2200
Horse of Busha
Long Rigg   cairn   1900   1800   1700   1600
2100
2000
③ Bram Rigg Top
2100
2000
1900
1800

Brown Moor

Long Rigg Gill   Long Rigg Beck

White Fell

Bram Rigg

1300
1200
1100
1000
900
800

Castley Knotts

① Calf Beck

tractor track

④ rocky cuttings   old sheepfold   1500
1400
1300

Seevy Rigg   1200
1100
1000

Calders Rigg

looking north

1000   900   800   700

gate

②

② Castley (farm)   700

Bram Rigg Beck   x sheepfold

800   900   700

sign post

Cookson's Tenement

Four Lane Ends

TODAY 6

SEDBERGH 3½

Chapel Beck

BIRKHAW FARM

The path descending Bram Rigg slants down to cross Bram Rigg Beck and continues distinctly to Birkhaw Farm. Use this path if bound for Sedbergh on foot. Otherwise return via Castley farm.

The first thing to do is to identify Four Lane Ends correctly. It is 3½ miles out of Sedbergh (Howgill Lane) and two-thirds of a mile beyond Howgill Church. (signpost at the corner).

Don't confuse CASTLEY with CAUTLEY!

MAP

9
(2)

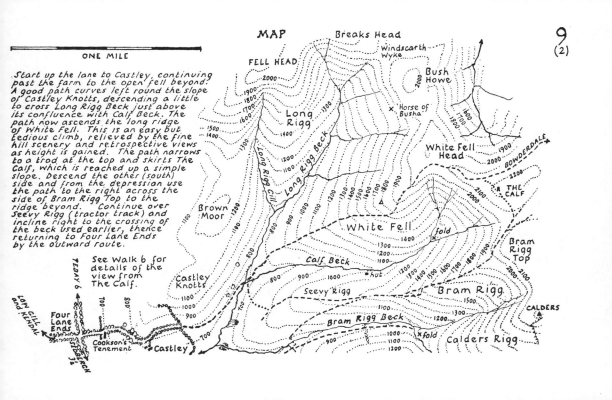

Start up the lane to Castley, continuing past the farm to the open fell beyond. A good path curves left round the slope of Castley Knotts, descending a little to cross Long Rigg Beck just above its confluence with Calf Beck. The path now ascends the long ridge of White Fell. This is an easy but tedious climb, relieved by the fine hill scenery and retrospective views as height is gained. The path narrows to a trod at the top and skirts The Calf, which is reached up a simple slope. Descend the other (south) side and from the depression use the path to the right across the side of Bram Rigg Top to the ridge beyond. Continue over Seevy Rigg (tractor track) and incline right to the crossing of the beck used earlier, thence returning to Four Lane Ends by the outward route.

See Walk 6 for details of the view from The Calf.

Breaks Head
FELL HEAD
Windscarth Wyke
Bush Howe
Horse of Busha
Long Rigg
White Fell Head
BOWDERDALE
THE CALF
Brown Moor
White Fell
fold
Bram Rigg Top
Calf Beck
hut
Bram Rigg
Seevy Rigg
CALDERS
Castley Knotts
Bram Rigg Beck
fold
Calders Rigg
Four Lane Ends
Cookson's Tenement
Castley
LOW GILL and KENDAL
TO DAY 6

above : The path from Castley curves left around the slopes of Castley Knotts to reveal an intimate view of the central mass. On the left is Bush Howe and its 'Horse'; in the middle is White Fell with the path clearly seen ascending its ridge; on the right is The Calf with Bram Rigg coming into the picture below it.

right : As the path descends to cross Long Rigg Beck, Fell Head comes into view, left, at the head of the valley. On the right are the ridges of Bush Howe, White Fell and Bram Rigg, separated by eroded ravines bringing down tributary becks. The main stream becomes Chapel Beck, flowing by Howgill Church to join the River Lune.

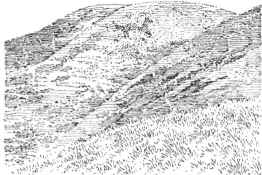

above : Clearly visible from the Castley path as
it approaches the crossing of Long Rigg
Beck is the "Horse (or Black Horse) of
Busha' (or Bushaw or Bush Howe)" below
the distant skyline of Bush Howe, and it
comes into sight much nearer from the
ridge of White Fell (as here illustrated).
It is not a shape artificially cut into the
fellside but is merely a patch of stones
naturally fallen into this position.

left : On the small area of flat ground near the
confluence of Long Rigg Beck and Cals Beck
are half a dozen small circles of stones. It
is thought that these are the remains of the
hut dwellings of the very early settlers in
the district. In the background Long Rigg
rises to the summit of Fell Head.

FELL HEAD AND THE CALF

6¾ miles

FROM BECK HOUSES (OR FAIRMILE GATE)

This high-level traverse of the plateau splendidly reveals the topographical details of the Howgills.

THE CALF 2220' ④

White Fell Head

Breaks Head

Bush Howe ③

FELL HEAD 2070' ②

2100'
2000'
1900'
1800'
1700'
1600'
1500'
1400'
fold

path goes on to Black Force col

Blake Ridge ②

Linghaw

1600'
1500'
1400'
1300'
1200'
1100'
1000'
900'

2045'

Windscarth Wyke

Horse of Busha

1900'
1800'
1700'

1800'
1700'

direct route

1600'

Long Rigg

Long Rigg Beck

White Fell

good view of the Horse ⑤

1500'
1400'
1300'

Dry Gill

blind Gill

Fairmile Beck

① Whins End

1200'

leave the path here

1200'
1100'
1000'
900'

col ⑥

fold

Brown Moor

alternative start

parking places

1000'
900'

Whins (farm)

800'

Beck Houses Gate (three, actually)

Calf Beck

The mileage is measured from Beck Houses. The distance from Fairmile Gate is slightly less.

milestone

barn

Fairmile Gate (cattle grid)

Note the old milestone (very ancient).

800'
700'

Beck Houses (farm)

fall

old lane

cross the beck

sheepfolds

Castley Knotts

800'
700'

See Walk 6 for details of the view from The Calf.

ROAD

This road is laid on the course of the Roman road to Low Borrow Bridge.

Gate House (farm)

CASTLEY

looking north-east

At Beck Houses starts one of the very few _public_ footpaths into the hills: an excellent terrace-walk high on the flanks of Fell Head and leading to the top of Black Force. This path can be used as a start (and finish) to the walk here described, and is the best way if approaching from Sedbergh on foot. The first section from the farmhouse to the intake gate, however, is untidy, the lane connecting the two being wet and overgrown. Pass to the right of the house, through a gate, and cross the beck 100 yards further (no footbridge), thence proceeding up the side of the field outside the confines of the old lane. From the intake gate onwards the way is clear.

Motorists will have the problem of finding space to leave their cars, the road being narrow, and, to avoid begging permission to park at the farm, it is a much better plan to continue north to the open fell beyond Fairmile Gate, where there is ample room on the verges. Then walk up Fairmile Beck, crossing it to the easy slope of Whins End, at the top of which the path from Beck Houses is joined. Actually this is a better start than the other, more straightforward and simple, while avoiding farmyard perils and disturbances. (An obvious and shorter alternative for motorists of abounding energy is to climb straight up and over Linghaw to the col. This is a steeper route, although not in the category of the south face of Annapurna).

Where the routes converge on Whins End a direct climb up the ridge to Fell Head can be made on a slight track, but if time is not an enemy prefer to go along the Black Force path to the Linghaw col, there turning up a simple incline, Blake Ridge, to the summit. From Fell Head onwards the route lies along the grassy plateau to The Calf, keeping to the height of land. The immediate surroundings are without interest but the views down into the ravines on both sides are very impressive. From The Calf return to White Fell Head and descend its southwest ridge on a good path (bound for Castley) but near its foot incline right for the confluence of Long Rigg Beck and Long Rigg Gill. Ascend the latter for

Fell Head, from Beck Houses

Fell Head, from Fairmile Beck

a third of a mile in colourful surroundings of heather and bracken and bilberry before climbing left to the pleasant col between Brown Moor and Fell Head, from which the Beck Houses path is quickly regained. Follow it down to the farm and the road (but if aiming for a car parked near to Fairmile Gate, turn right along the path, climbing a little to Whins End being making a beeline to it). If bound for Sedbergh on foot, omit this final section and continue on the path to Castley.

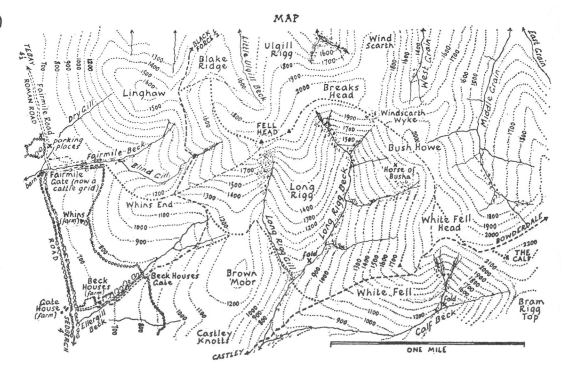

ONE MILE

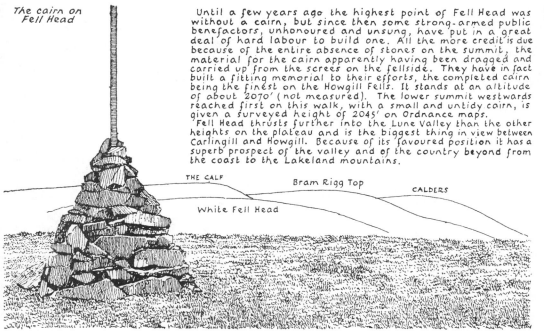

The cairn on Fell Head

Until a few years ago the highest point of Fell Head was without a cairn, but since then some strong-armed public benefactors, unhonoured and unsung, have put in a great deal of hard labour to build one. All the more credit is due because of the entire absence of stones on the summit, the material for the cairn apparently having been dragged and carried up from the screes on the fellside. They have in fact built a fitting memorial to their efforts, the completed cairn being the finest on the Howgill Fells. It stands at an altitude of about 2070' (not measured). The lower summit westwards reached first on this walk, with a small and untidy cairn, is given a surveyed height of 2045' on Ordnance maps.

Fell Head thrusts further into the Lune Valley than the other heights on the plateau and is the biggest thing in view between Carlingill and Howgill. Because of its favoured position it has a superb prospect of the valley and of the country beyond from the coast to the Lakeland mountains.

THE CALF

Bram Rigg Top

CALDERS

White Fell Head

BLACK FORCE

FROM CARLINGILL BRIDGE

3½ miles

looking southeast

Spectacular
scenery of
geological
interest,
reached only by
rough scrambling.
Apart from this,
an easy walk.

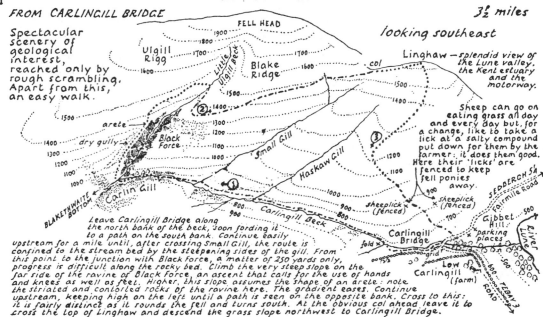

Linghaw — splendid view of
the Lune valley,
the Kent estuary
and the
motorway.

Sheep can go on
eating grass all day
and every day but, for
a change, like to take a
lick at a salty compound
put down for them by the
farmer: it does them good.
Here their 'licks' are
fenced to keep
fell ponies
away.

Leave Carlingill Bridge along
the north bank of the beck, soon fording it
to a path on the south bank. Continue easily
upstream for a mile until, after crossing Small Gill, the route is
confined to the stream bed by the steepening sides of the gill. From
this point to the junction with Black Force, a matter of 250 yards only,
progress is difficult along the rocky bed. Climb the very steep slope on the
far side of the ravine of Black Force, an ascent that calls for the use of hands
and knees as well as feet. Higher, this slope assumes the shape of an arete: note
the striated and contorted rocks of the ravine here. The gradient eases. Continue
upstream, keeping high on the left until a path is seen on the opposite bank. Cross to this:
it is fairly distinct as it rounds the fell and turns south. At the obvious col ahead leave it to
cross the top of Linghaw and descend the grass slope northwest to Carlingill Bridge.

MAP

11
(2)

ONE MILE

Northbound travellers on the motorway, as they swing round into the valley of the River Lune from the moors of Killington, have already had the Howgill range in sight before them for some miles, but as they take the long left curve the view to the north gradually opens up to reveal what is, by common consent, the grandest prospect the motorway has to offer: that of the Lune Gorge, between the Whinfell Ridge on the left and the northern Howgills (although 'gorge' is too extravagant a name for it).

It is a measure of the quality of the landscape that (unusually for a motorway) a 'pull-off' to a lay-by has been provided for motorists who wish to stop and feast their eyes upon the scenery.

Gibbet Hill is reputedly a place where stealers of sheep were hung in the good old days.

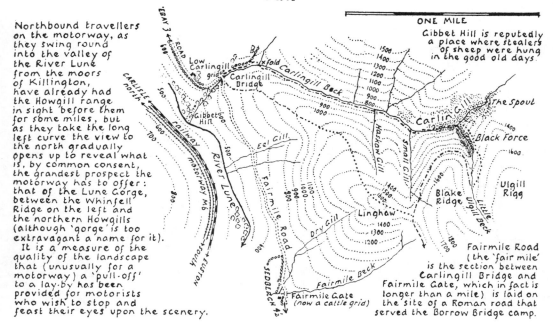

Fairmile Road (the 'fair mile' is the section between Carlingill Bridge and Fairmile Gate, which in fact is longer than a mile) is laid on the site of a Roman road that served the Borrow Bridge camp.

Carlingill Bridge

The lower reaches of Carlin Gill

The malformed keystones and secondary arch under the bridge indicate an extension and a widening of the original structure.

The view is upstream to the ravine of Black Force (arrowed). The beck marks the boundary between Westmorland (left) and Yorkshire.

Black Force

The ravine of Black Force
*as seen from the
upper reaches
of Carlin Gill*

This walk cannot be done if the beck is in flood.
A half-mile section is a battle against nature in
the raw and ends in a desperate scramble.
Nonagenarians should think twice before
attempting it.

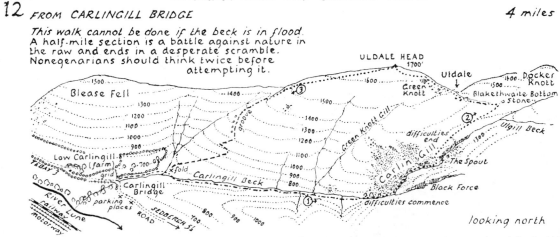

looking north

Leave Carlingill Bridge along the north bank of the beck, soon fording it to a path on the south bank; this is then followed upstream for an easy and pleasant mile. After passing the second tributary coming in on the right, the route is confined to the narrow rocky bed of the beck by very steep slopes on both flanks and progress becomes a rough scramble. The cascade of Black Force appears on the right in impressive style, the way continuing up the main ravine until an unclimbable 30' waterfall (The Spout), partly hidden behind a steep rib of rock, is reached. The only escape is up a stony crack to the left of the rib — a steep scramble — to easier ground above the fall. Now traverse grass slopes to the green hollow of Blakethwaite Bottom, where turn left rather steeply to the broad top of Uldale Head, a fine viewpoint. Cross the top in the direction of Blease Fell to the head of a stream, where lines of rushes indicate a grooved drove road that leads pleasantly downhill to Carlingill Beck at a sheepfold with the bridge in sight ahead

MAP

12
(2)

The 1600' contour on Uldale Head is assumed
and should not be taken as gospel.
See page 4.

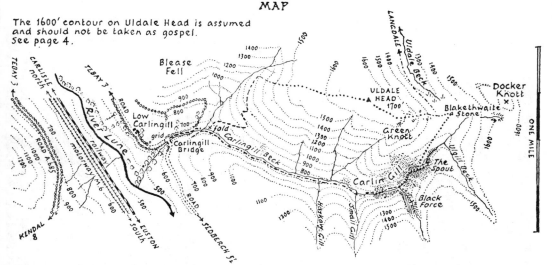

The deep cutting of Carlin Gill and its fine surrounding hills have excited the attention of passing
railway travellers for over a century, and now they appeal no less to travellers along the new
motorway. The best place of departure from the motorway for those who wish to visit the area
is the Tebay access, proceeding thence along the Kendal road to Low Borrow Bridge where a road
for Carlingill (and Howgill and Sedbergh) turns off on the left. The Killington access (on the road
between Kendal and Sedbergh) is a less convenient point of departure.

left: *The upper reaches of Carlin Gill as seen from above Black Force.*

below:
The Spout

The summit, looking east.

Blakethwaite Stone
(see Walk 15
for a note about
this boulder)

The height of Uldale Head

He is a bold man who questions the triangulations of the Ordnance surveyors, for they are the experts, meticulous in all their work and wellnigh infallible. Yet surely they are guilty of an incredible oversight in recording the altitude of Uldale Head as 1553' on their 1", 2½" and 6" maps. From the summit, the neighbouring Blease Fell (1556'), Hare Shaw (1548') and Rispa Pike (1554') are well below eye level. Across Blakethwaite Bottom is Docker Knott (with a 1700' contour), which appears to be no higher and is overtopped some 200 feet by Simon's Seat (1925') behind. The climb up from the Blakethwaite Stone (1325') involves a considerably greater amount of ascent than the 230 feet suggested by the maps and must be nearer 400.

For the purposes of this chapter, the height of Uldale Head is assumed, with tongue in cheek, to be 1700' approximately. The truth will not be known until the next survey. By that time the author will be past caring what the height of Uldale Head is.

PROOF (?)

If Uldale Head is 1553' only the tip of Simon's Seat would be visible above Docker Knott

If Uldale Head is 1700' the top 200' of Simon's Seat would be visible above Docker Knott

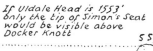

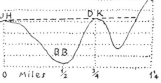

UH : Uldale Head
BB : Blakethwaite Bottom
DK : Docker Knott
SS : Simon's Seat

The vertical scale is greatly exaggerated

It is not suggested that the O.S. do their sums this way.

— and it is!

Q.E.D.

STOP PRESS : The attention of the Ordnance Survey having been drawn to their apparent error, they kindly sent a surveyor to check the altitude. He found it to be 1747 feet approximately.

TEBAY GILL, BLEASE FELL AND HARE SHAW

looking
south-east

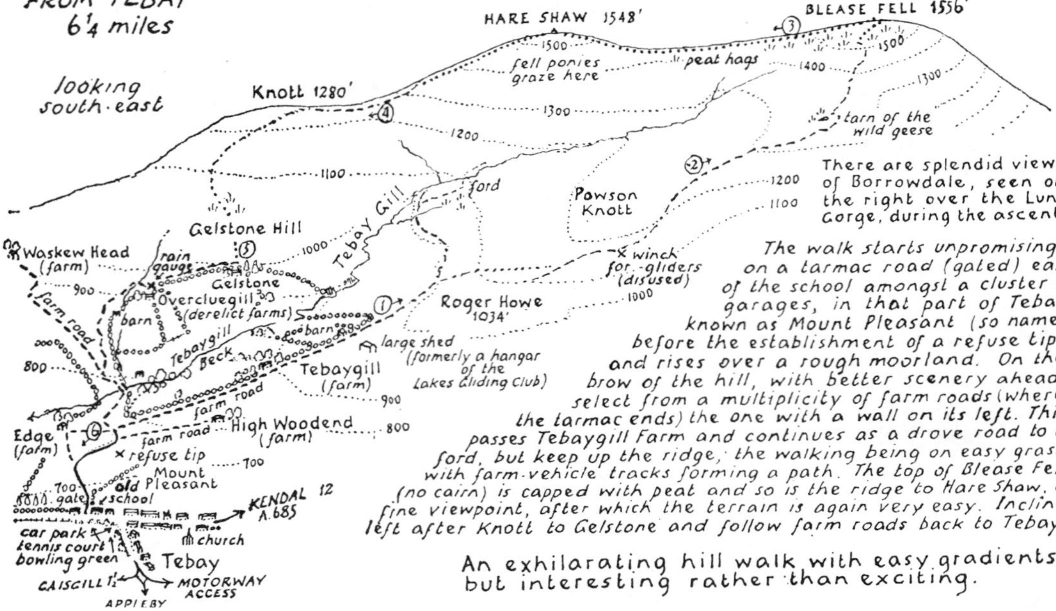

There are splendid views of Borrowdale, seen on the right over the Lune Gorge, during the ascent.

The walk starts unpromisingly on a tarmac road (gated) east of the school amongst a cluster of garages, in that part of Tebay known as Mount Pleasant (so named before the establishment of a refuse tip), and rises over a rough moorland. On the brow of the hill, with better scenery ahead, select from a multiplicity of farm roads (where the tarmac ends) the one with a wall on its left. This passes Tebaygill Farm and continues as a drove road to a ford, but keep up the ridge, the walking being on easy grass with farm-vehicle tracks forming a path. The top of Blease Fell (no cairn) is capped with peat and so is the ridge to Hare Shaw, a fine viewpoint, after which the terrain is again very easy. Incline left after Knott to Gelstone and follow farm roads back to Tebay.

An exhilarating hill walk with easy gradients, but interesting rather than exciting.

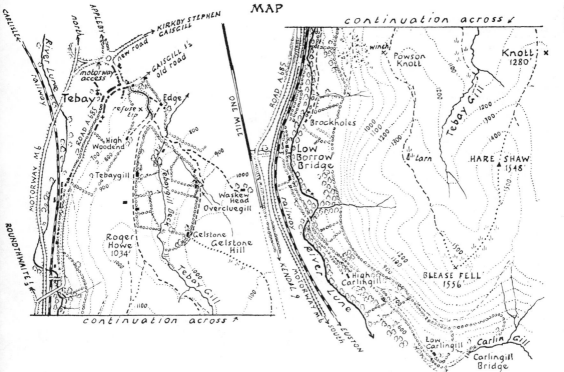

MAP

continuation across ↓

CARLISLE

APPLEBY

north

KIRKBY STEPHEN
GAISGILL

new road

GAISGILL 1½
old road

motorway
access

Tebay

Edge

refuse ✗ tip

High
Woodend

Tebaygill

Waskew Head
Overcluegill

Roger Howe
1034

Gelstone

Gelstone
Hill

Tebay Gill

River Lune

railway

MOTORWAY M6

ROAD A685

ROUNDTHWAITE 3

ONE MILE

ROAD A685

KENDAL 9

MOTORWAY M6 SOUTH

railway

EUSTON

River Lune

winch

Powson
Knott

Knott
1280 ✗

Tebay Gill

Brockholes

Low
Borrow
Bridge

Tarn

HARE SHAW
1548

BLEASE FELL
1556

High
Carlingill

Low
Carlingill

Carlin Gill

Carlingill
Bridge

continuation across ↑

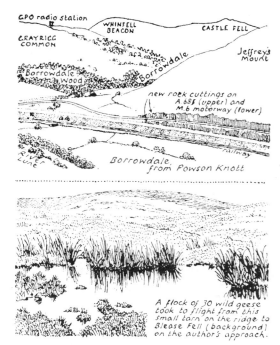

GPO radio station

WHINFELL BEACON

CASTLE FELL

CRAYRIGG COMMON

Borrowdale

Jeffrey's Mount

Borrowdale Wood

new rock cuttings on A.685 (upper) and M.6 motorway (lower)

River Lune

railway

Borrowdale, from Powson Knott

A flock of 30 wild geese took to flight from this small tarn on the ridge to Blease Fell (background) on the author's approach.

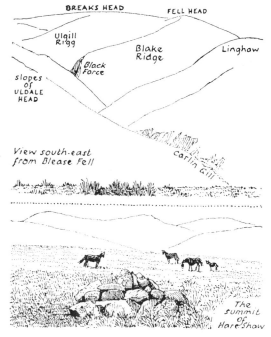

BREAKS HEAD

FELL HEAD

Ulgill Rigg

Blake Ridge

Linghaw

slopes of ULDALE HEAD

Black Force

View south-east from Blease Fell

Carlin Gill

The summit of Hare Shaw

Gelstone

The ruins of Overcluegill

Bridge over Tebaygill Beck

An excellent exercise for the legs on
very easy gradients. The distant scenery
is better than that in the near vicinity.

RISPA PIKE 1554'

Uldale
End

Eller Gill

looking southeast

Gaisgill
— lots of
car-parking
space (free).

The new road at Gaisgill (giving direct
access to the motorway) is laid on the
permanent(!) way of the former
Tebay - Barnard Castle railway.

A narrow overgrown lane turning off the old Tebay road
100 yards west of the Methodist chapel leads to pastures
rising to the farm of Gill Hole, beyond which a tarmac
road is joined and followed to the next farm, where it
ends. (More simply, this tarmac road can be followed
directly from the old Tebay road 400 yards west of the
chapel). The way up the valley, keeping alongside the
intake wall, is now clear on an excellent track, which
continues distinctly beyond the wall to end finally at a
large sheepfold after descending to, and crossing, the
valley stream. Now, on a diminishing path that peters
out, ascend the long grass slope half-left to reach the
depression south of Rispa Pike, the top of which is then
within easy reach. A wall-shelter adorns the summit. A
fine view opens up, particularly northwards. Below,
running up into the hills, is the valley of Uldale.

Return along the gentle decline of the north ridge, where a tractor track will soon be picked up; this descends
to the intake wall on the east side of the valley, joining the overgrown cart-track that served the now-derelict
farm of Raw Busk. Keep alongside the wall: the track improves and is joined by another coming from Long
Gills before descending to the farm of Ellergill. Gaisgill is a field's distance beyond.

MAP

14
(2)

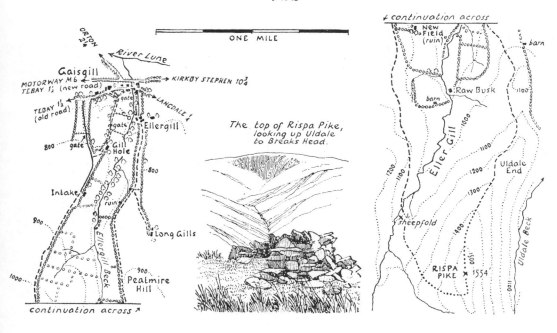

ONE MILE

ORTON 2¾

River Lune

Gaisgill

MOTORWAY M6
TEBAY 1½ (new road)   ← KIRKBY STEPHEN 10¾

TEBAY 1½ (old road)   LANGDALE 1

gate

800   gate   Ellergill

gate   Gill
             Hole

Intake   800

900   ruin

Ellergill Beck

1000   Long Gills

900

Peatmire
Hill

continuation across →

The top of Rispa Pike,
looking up Uldale
to Breaks Head.

← continuation across

New Field (ruin)   barn

barn   Raw Busk   1100

1200   1100   1000   Eller Gill   1100

1100   1200   Uldale End

1300

sheepfold   1400

1500   1100

RISPA
PIKE   × 1554   1100   Uldale Beck

Leaving Langdale school (car parking space), the first objective is Long Gills, a farm hidden by trees on the low ridge west of the beck. Reach it through the facing gate at the road-end, alongside a farm; here a muddy walled lane with two gates turns sharp right, then left, to a bridge across the beck. Slanting up the opposite bank amongst trees is an overgrown cart-track that enters a field at a gate with Long Gills now seen ahead. Cross the field to it (there is little evidence of the cart-track here, the farm now being served instead by a rough road from Ellergill). More gates at the farm admit to the open fell on the right of the wall. Now the route is straightforward, on a fair track alongside the intake wall. Rounding Uldale End, where the wall turns down to the valley bottom, the view ahead opens up to reveal the two ascending ridges of Middleton and Hand Lake, with Churn Gill deep between them, Langdale Beck away to the left backed by Langdale Knott, and the valley of Uldale straight ahead. The track leaves the wall and descends slightly into Uldale. Follow the stream to its source in the green amphitheatre of Blakethwaite Bottom. A steepish climb left up the side of a fluted gully leads to the small neat top of Docker Knott. Ahead, the great dome of Simon's Seat is now seen prominently for the first time, but is unfortunately severed from this viewpoint by the deep trench of Churngill Beck, and it will be obvious that if this latter stream had been followed up instead of Uldale Beck the descent to it would have been avoided. It is no use crying over spilt milk, and in any case Uldale is the pleasanter approach, so slant down to the right to ease the gradient, cross the stream, contour around the opposite bank, cross a tributary and then climb up the grassy slope of Simon's Seat to the peaty summit, which disappointingly has no cairn and no material at hand for making one except for sheep-droppings, which lack the necessary attribute of permanency.

continued ↗

A fine expedition into the wild
fastnesses of upper Langdale;
contrasting scenery;
mostly easy walking.

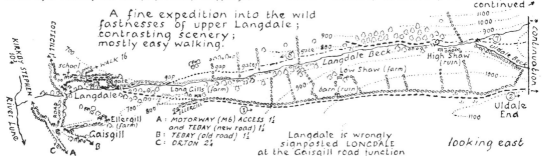

A: MOTORWAY (M6) ACCESS 1¼
and TEBAY (new road) 1½
B: TEBAY (old road) 1½
C: ORTON 2¼

Langdale is wrongly
signposted LONGDALE
at the Gaisgill road junction

looking east

continued
From Simon's Seat, the Middleton ridge used for the return journey is seen curving away half-left, identifiable by its white survey column. This two-mile ridge leads down very pleasantly to the floor of the valley; from the column a tractor track (probably made during the construction of the column) may be used. The view ahead of the lower part of the valley is charming, and an old arched bridge at the foot of the ridge, crossing Langdale Beck near its confluence with Uldale Beck, is a delightful surprise. The ruins of High Shaw, seen down-valley, could formerly be reached by a path on the left bank after fording Uldale Beck, but a locked and barbed gate bars this approach. Instead, go down the right bank, rounding a wall above the stream and so join the old cart-track to High Shaw at another bridge. Keeping to the right bank, follow this cart-track downstream in a wooded glen, and when it starts to climb out of the valley leave it to continue along the beckside through a succession of fields, climbing three gates and after passing through a wall-gap gain the intimate bank of the stream at another wall-gap closed by a bed-end and so rejoin the outward route at the first bridge. Your car is now only five minutes distant.

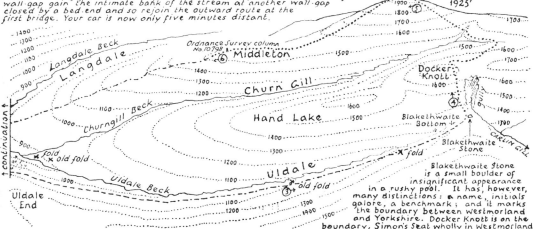

SIMON'S SEAT
1925'

Ordnance Survey column No 10798

⑥ Middleton

Docker Knott

Churn Gill

Hand Lake

Blakethwaite Bottom

Blakethwaite Stone

CARLIN GILL

Langdale Beck

Langdale

Churngill Beck

Uldale

Uldale Beck

fold   old fold

old fold

fold

Uldale End

continuation

Blakethwaite Stone is a small boulder of insignificant appearance in a rushy pool. It has, however, many distinctions: a name, initials galore, a benchmark; and it marks the boundary between Westmorland and Yorkshire. Docker Knott is on the boundary, Simon's Seat wholly in Westmorland

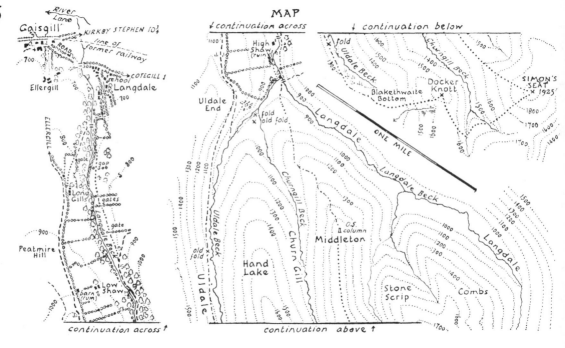

MAP

Of the five northern valleys, Langdale is the central one, the longest, the most attractive, and, by reason of its several major tributaries and ridges, much the most complicated in structure. The lower part is well wooded, narrow, and scenically very pleasant, the beck being charming; then, in open country, the main stream is joined by three considerable feeders separated by lofty ridges that culminate in the high dome of Simon's Seat, the dominant feature of Langdale. The main valley, however, runs much further into the heart of the hills in a great curve before finally dividing into three branches, the middle one extending to The Calf, the apex of the Howgills.

Bowderdale

Hazelgill
Knott

West
Fell

Langdale

East Grain

Middle Grain

Grains

THE
CALF

Langdale
Knott

Combs

1500

Simon's
Seat

Cobles

West Grain

2000

White
Fell Head

Langdale Beck

Stone
Scrip

Middleton

1500

Breaks Head

Churngill Beck

Churn Gill

Docker Knott

River Lune

Langdale

1000

Hand Lake

Uldale Beck

NORTH

ONE MILE

Watershed:
xxxxxxxx

Eller Gill

Uldale

Uldale Head

Rispa Pike

Langdale should be studied carefully on the map before being explored. The watercourses are deepset between lofty heights, so that from no one point can the topography be fully appreciated, while the similarity of the terrain and lack of distinguishing features add to the sense of confusion that must inevitably arise unless the general lie of the land is memorised in advance and the map frequently consulted during the course of any walks undertaken in this area.

The start from Langdale School
The route goes through the gate at the road end

Simon's Seat   Hand Lake

Churn Gill, from the path on Uldale End

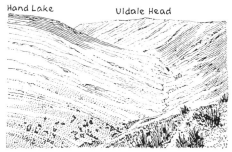

Hand Lake   Uldale Head

Uldale, from the path on Uldale End

The summit of Simon's Seat, looking south

The view from Simon's Seat

The view southwards is restricted by higher fells buttressing The Calf, but its intimate detail of upper Langdale is good. In other directions the panorama is widespread. In the west the Lakeland hills extend from the Coniston range to Blencathra and Carrock Fell. Cross Fell, Mickle Fell and a long sweep of the Pennines appear in the north, while Wildboar Fell, Swarth Fell and Baugh Fell are seen eastwards peeping over depressions in the long Bowderdale ridge.

Old footbridge, Langdale Beck

(omitted from Ordnance maps)

Ordnance Survey column on Middleton Simon's Seat in the background

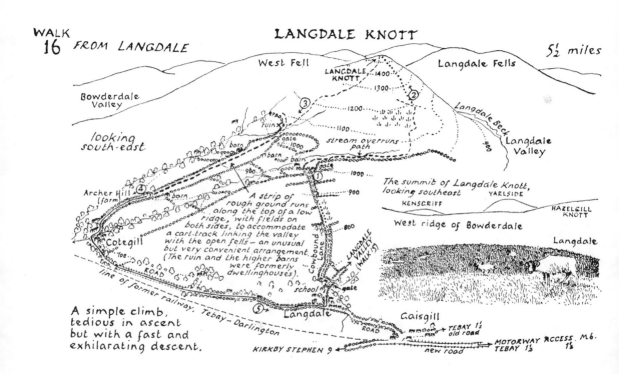

WALK 16 FROM LANGDALE

LANGDALE KNOTT

5½ miles

West Fell

LANGDALE KNOTT 1400

Langdale Fells

Bowderdale Valley

1300

looking south-east

1200

Langdale Beck

1100

stream overruns path

Langdale Valley

900

ruin ×

barn

gate

1000

barn barn

Archer Hill (farm)

barn

900

1000

900

The summit of Langdale Knott, looking southeast

KENSCRIFF   YARLSIDE

HAZELGILL KNOTT

West ridge of Bowderdale

Cotegill

A strip of rough ground runs along the top of a low ridge, with fields on both sides, to accommodate a cart-track linking the valley with the open fells — an unusual but very convenient arrangement. (The ruin and the higher barns were formerly dwellinghouses).

800

Cowbound Lane

LANGDALE VALLEY (WALK 5)

Langdale

700

ROAD

line of former railway, Tebay-Darlington

school

gate

A simple climb, tedious in ascent but with a fast and exhilarating descent.

Langdale

Gaisgill

ROAD

KIRKBY STEPHEN 9

new road

TEBAY 1½ old road

MOTORWAY ACCESS M6.
TEBAY 1½   1½

MAP

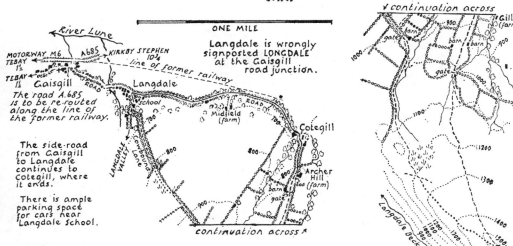

ONE MILE

Langdale is wrongly
signposted LONGDALE
at the Gaisgill
road junction.

← River Lune

MOTORWAY M6 A685 KIRKBY STEPHEN
TEBAY 1½ ← 10½
———— line of former railway
TEBAY 1½
Gaisgill

The road A.685
is to be re-routed
along the line of
the former railway.

Langdale

The side-road
from Gaisgill
to Langdale
continues to
Cotegill, where
it ends.

There is ample
parking space
for cars near
Langdale School.

school

ROAD

Midfield
(farm)

LANGDALE VALLEY

Cowbound Lane

700

800

800

700

Cotegill

barn

Archer
Hill
(farm)

gate

barn

900

continuation across ↑

↓ continuation across

Gills
(farm)

900

gate

barn barn

1000

900

gate

1000

1100

1000

1200

1300

Langdale Deck

1200
1000
900

1300

1400

1500

LANGDALE KNOTT
1560'

From the school, walk up the lane for 100 yards to two gates. Take the one on the left,
not the one facing, and proceed up a green road that rejoices in the name of Cowbound Lane.
After a mile a small valley crosses the route : turn right here alongside a stream that disputes
the right of way. A tractor track turns up the grassy slope : follow this around a morass and then aim
directly up the very easy ridge ahead to the top of Langdale Knott, which has no cairn. The central mass
of the Howgill Fells appears in front, intimately and strikingly seen. Only northwards is the view open to
the far distance, and this can be enjoyed fully on the long gentle gradient of the descent to Cotegill. A
distinct tractor track leaves the summit and leads straight down to the intake wall, continuing forward
along a strip of rough ground between cultivated fields to Archer Hill farm, where tarmac is again reached.
A pleasant road, rich in autumn berries (rose, sloe, elder, hawthorn) is followed back to Langdale.

BOWDERDALE, THE CALF AND WEST FELL

FROM BOWDERDALE FOOT

12 miles

This is the longest direct ascent of The Calf, which is more distant from the road at Bowderdale than from any other motor road around the perimeter of the Howgills, yet the route is an obvious one, the valley cutting straight and deep into the hills to the central plateau. The walk as described goes up the valley, emerging near its head to cross the plateau to The Calf, and returns down the long ridge bounding it on the west. It is a fine fast walk without any steep gradients, but lovers of drama will find the scenery monotonous while conceding that Bowderdale is a noble valley indeed.

A car parked at Bowderdale Foot is almost essential to the journey, the railway through the upper Lune valley having been closed and the bus service along the A.685 being too infrequent to be of much help. A walker who can contrive to reach Bowderdale Foot by other means (fair or foul) has, however, the advantage of being able to continue south beyond The Calf and so down to Sedbergh —a magnificent full-length traverse of the Howgills — or from The Calf he may descend to Cautley, the quickest way off to a meal and a public road.

The A.685 road connects Kirkby Stephen with Tebay and the M6 motorway access. The side road to Bowderdale leaves it one mile west of Newbiggin on Lune.

RANDYGILL TOP 2047'

boulders and scree

Bowderdale

bield

old fold

West Fell

tractor track

barn and sheepfolds

Bowderdale Beck

Bowderdale (farm)

A.685 ROAD

gates

gate

to River Lune

Bowderdale Foot

cattle grid

ROAD → FLAKEBRIDGE

Bowderdale is locally pronounced Boother-dl.

looking southeast

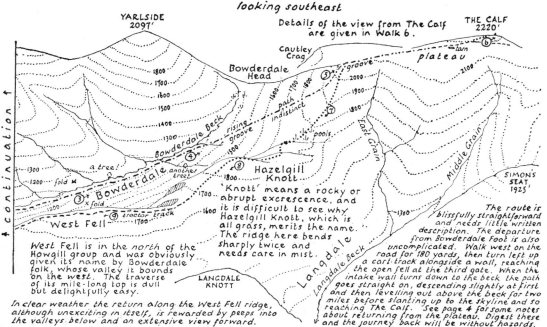

Details of the view from The Calf are given in Walk 6.

YARLSIDE 2097'

THE CALF 2220'

Cautley Crag

Bowderdale Head

tarn plateau

← continuation ↑

1800 1700 1600 1500 1400 1300

Bowderdale Beck

rising groove

Path indistinct

groove

pools

East Grain

Middle Grain

2100 2000 1900 1800

SIMON'S SEAT 1925'

1300 1200 · fold ✕

a tree!

1300

3 ✕ fold

another tree!

Hazelgill Knott

1800 1700

1600

1700

West Fell

tractor track

*'Knott' means a rocky or
abrupt excrescence, and
it is difficult to see why
Hazelgill Knott, which is
all grass, merits the name.
The ridge here bends
sharply twice and
needs care in mist.*

1300

*West Fell is in the north of the
Howgill group and was obviously
given its name by Bowderdale
folk, whose valley it bounds
on the west. The traverse
of its mile-long top is dull
but delightfully easy.*

LANGDALE KNOTT

Langdale Beck

*The route is
blissfully straightforward
and needs little written
description. The departure
from Bowderdale Foot is also
uncomplicated. Walk west on the
road for 180 yards, then turn left up
a cart-track alongside a wall, reaching
the open fell at the third gate. When the
intake wall turns down to the beck the path
goes straight on, descending slightly at first
and then levelling out above the beck for two
miles before slanting up to the skyline and so
reaching The Calf. See page 4 for some notes
about returning from the plateau. Digest these
and the journey back will be without hazards.*

*In clear weather the return along the West Fell ridge,
although unexciting in itself, is rewarded by peeps into
the valleys below and an extensive view forward.*

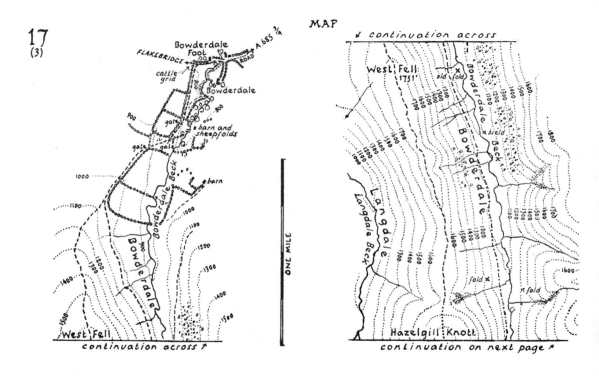

Bowderdale
Foot

FLAKEBRIDGE

A.685 ¾

ROAD

cattle
grid

Bowderdale

900

gate

barn and
sheepfolds

gate   gate

gate

1000

Bowderdale Beck

barn

1000

1100

1100

1200

Bowderdale

900

1300

1400

1300

1400

1500

1500

West Fell

continuation across ↑

ONE MILE

continuation across ↓

West Fell
1751'

old fold

Bowderdale Beck

1200
1300
1400
1500
1700

1200
1300
1500

field

1700

1800

1700

1800

Bowderdale

1700
1600
1500
1400
1300
1200
1000

Langdale Beck

1200
1300
1400
1500
1600

Langdale Beck

fold

fold

1600

1700
1600
1500
1400
1300
1200

Hazelgill Knott

continuation on next page →

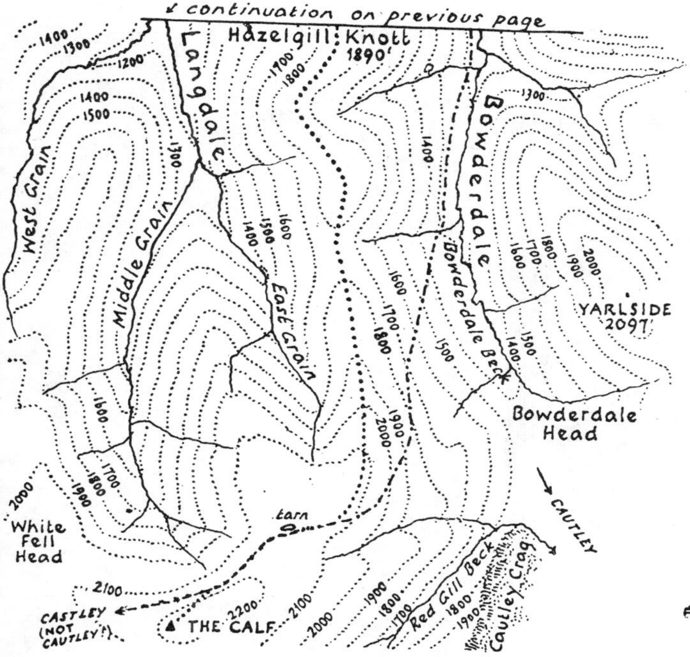

MAP

17
(4)

This map is extended beyond the immediate vicinity of the route in the neighbourhood of The Calf in order to show clearly the various ridges and valleys descending northwards from the central plateau. The similarity of the terrain and an absence of distinguishing landmarks make this section confusing, even in clear weather, without the safe guidance of a known path. Little difficulty will be experienced in ascent, but when descending the possibility of getting into a wrong valley is very real. When leaving The Calf for the ridge of Hazelgill Knott and West Fell, which is hidden behind a minor summit, take care not to get on a parallel ridge that descends into Langdale between Middle Grain and East Grain. To avoid this, return along the path used in the ascent until it starts to descend into Bowderdale, then contour around the minor summit and keep due north for Hazelgill Knott across a marshy depression.

ONE MILE

17
(5) Bowderdale Foot

Barn and sheepfolds,
Bowderdale Beck

The lower reaches of Bowderdale,
looking up the valley
to West Fell

FROM WEASDALE

RANDYGILL TOP AND GREEN BELL

6¼ miles

This circuit of the Weasdale valley
is a splendid walk, interesting
in its geography and excellent
in its far-reaching views.

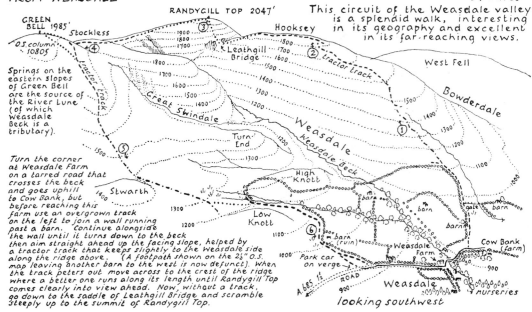

RANDYGILL TOP 2047'

GREEN
BELL 1985'   Stockless

O.S. column
10805

Springs on the
eastern slopes
of Green Bell
are the source of
the River Lune
(of which
Weasdale
Beck is a
tributary).

Great Swindale

Hooksey

Leathgill
Bridge

Tractor track

West Fell

Bowderdale

Weasdale

Weasdale Beck

Turn
End

Stwarth

High
Knott

Low
Knott

barn

barn

gate   barn

barn

Turn the corner
at Weasdale Farm
on a tarred road that
crosses the beck
and goes uphill
to Cow Bank, but
before reaching this
farm use an overgrown track
on the left to join a wall running
past a barn. Continue alongside
the wall until it turns down to the beck
then aim straight ahead up the facing slope, helped by
a tractor track that keeps slightly to the Weasdale side
along the ridge above. (A footpath shown on the 2½" O.S.
map leaving another barn to the west is now defunct). When
the track peters out move across to the crest of the ridge
where a better one runs along its length until Randygill Top
comes clearly into view ahead. Now, without a track,
go down to the saddle of Leathgill Bridge and scramble
steeply up to the summit of Randygill Top.

barn
(ruin)

Weasdale
Farm

Cow Bank
(farm)

Park car
on verge

A.685 1½

ROAD

Weasdale

nurseries

looking southwest

MAP

18
(2)

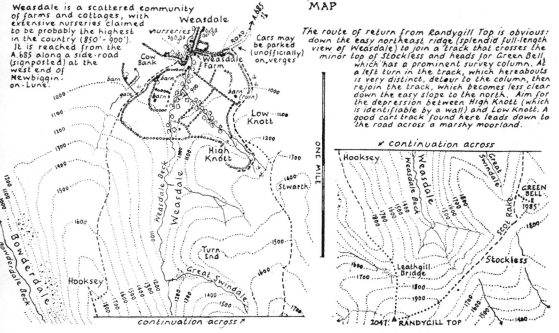

Weasdale is a scattered community of farms and cottages, with extensive nurseries claimed to be probably the highest in the country (850'–900'). It is reached from the A.685 along a side-road (signposted) at the west end of Newbiggin-on-Lune.

Weasdale

nurseries

Cow Bank

Cars may be parked (unofficially) on verges

Weasdale Farm

barn

barn

barn

barn (ruin)

gate

Low Knott

High Knott

Stwarth

Weasdale Beck

Weasdale

Bowderdale

Bowderdale Beck

Hooksey

Turn End

Great Swindale

ONE MILE

continuation across ↗

The route of return from Randygill Top is obvious: down the easy northeast ridge (splendid full-length view of Weasdale) to join a track that crosses the minor top of Stockless and heads for Green Bell, which has a prominent survey column. At a left turn in the track, which hereabouts is very distinct, detour to the column, then rejoin the track, which becomes less clear down the easy slope to the north. Aim for the depression between High Knott (which is identifiable by a wall) and Low Knott. A good cart track found here leads down to the road across a marshy moorland.

↗ continuation across

Hooksey

Weasdale Beck

Weasdale

Great Swindale

GREEN BELL 1985

Scot Rake

Leathgill Bridge

Stockless

2047' RANDYGILL TOP

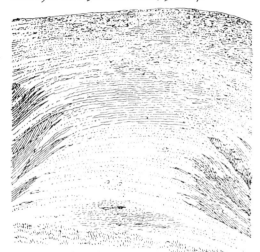

Leathgill Bridge is a natural
formation, not a manmade structure.
It is a splendid example of a saddle in a
depression of a ridge that serves as a pass
between the two valleys enclosing the ridge, in
this case Weasdale and Bowderdale but in fact
is rarely used as such because of its remoteness
from habitations and walkers' paths.

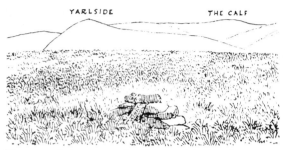

YARLSIDE   THE CALF

The summit is an unpretentious and featureless grass
dome, its only mystery being the source of the cairn
stones, which apparently have been hauled up there
from the Bowderdale flank, where outcrops occur, by
some visitor blessed with both enthusiasm and energy.

The view from Randygill Top

Whatever the other limitations of the summit, there can
be no denying its excellence as a viewpoint.   It is the
highest point of the Howgills along its degree of latitude
and therefore overtops the other fells in the group both
to west and east, while to the north the views are also
unrestricted by higher ground and very extensive.
Pride of place must go to the Lakeland skyline, which
extends from the Coniston range to Carrock Fell without
interruption.   Ingleborough and Whernside are in view
and there are glimpses of the Wensleydale and Wharfedale
hills beyond the wild Boar Fell and Baugh Fell massifs. Cross
Fell closes the horizon to the north.

*looking down Weasdale .
from the head of the valley*

The summit of Green Bell

THE CALF

YARLSIDE   RANDYGILL
                                          TOP

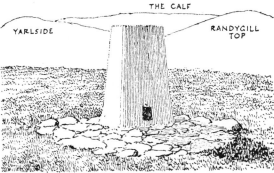

Ponies on the slopes of Green Bell

P.S.   Never offer titbits
         to grazing animals!

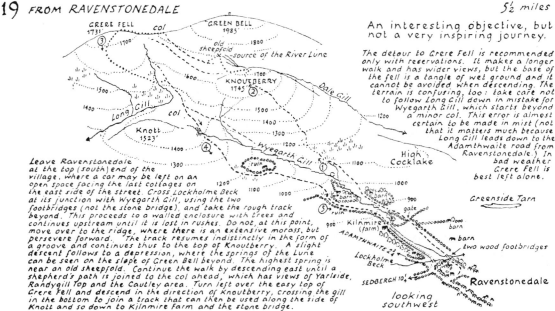

An interesting objective, but not a very inspiring journey.

The detour to Grere Fell is recommended only with reservations. It makes a longer walk and has wider views, but the base of the fell is a tangle of wet ground and it cannot be avoided when descending. The terrain is confusing, too: take care not to follow Long Gill down in mistake for Wyegarth Gill, which starts beyond a minor col. This error is almost certain to be made in mist (not that it matters much because Long Gill leads down to the Adamthwaite road from Ravenstonedale.) In bad weather Grere Fell is best left alone.

Leave Ravenstonedale at the top (south) end of the village, where a car may be left on an open space facing the last cottages on the east side of the street. Cross Lockholme Beck at its junction with Wyegarth Gill, using the two footbridges (not the stone bridge), and take the rough track beyond. This proceeds to a walled enclosure with trees and continues upstream until it is lost in rushes. Do not, at this point, move over to the ridge, where there is an extensive morass, but persevere forward. The track resumes indistinctly in the form of a groove and continues thus to the top of Knoutberry. A slight descent follows to a depression, where the springs of the Lune can be seen on the slope of Green Bell beyond. The highest spring is near an old sheepfold. Continue the walk by descending east until a shepherd's path is joined to the col ahead, which has views of Yarlside, Randygill Top and the Cautley area. Turn left over the easy top of Grere Fell and descend in the direction of Knoutberry, crossing the gill in the bottom to join a track that can then be used along the side of Knott and so down to Kilmire Farm and the stone bridge.

MAP

19
(2)

High Cocklake, between Dale Gill (west) and Wyegarth Gill (east), is the first pronounced rise on the watershed between the River Lune and the River Eden. The Lune starts its journey as Dale Gill, becoming Greenside Beck and later Dry Sike before assuming the name of the Lune at Newbiggin. Wyegarth Gill joins Lockholme Beck to flow into Scandal Beck, which reaches the Eden near Kirkby Stephen.

Ravenstonedale (locally *Rassendl*) is one of Westmorland's loveliest villages. In the vicinity of the church particularly the scene is charming, but the whole place has a most delightful air of rural serenity and dignity. Besides which you can get ham and egg teas at the King's Head, on the A.685.

Knoutberry is the highest point on the watershed ridge. The name is a local one for *cloudberry*, but this lovely moorland plant was not seen on the occasion of the author's visit (in winter).

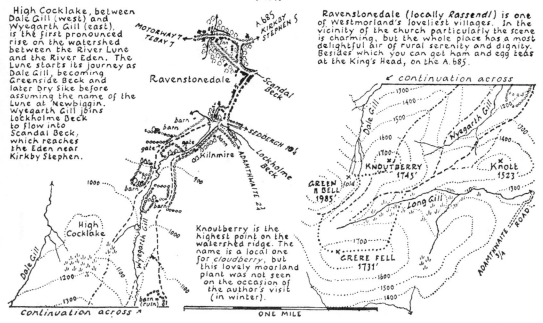

ONE MILE

continuation across →
← continuation across
continuation across ↑

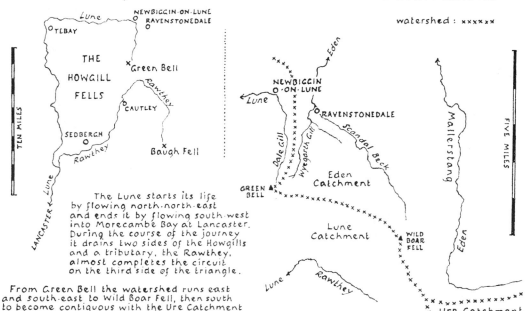

The course of the Lune

The Lune and Eden watershed

watershed : xxxxxx

THE HOWGILL FELLS

TEBAY

Lune

NEWBIGGIN-ON-LUNE
RAVENSTONEDALE

×Green Bell

CAUTLEY

Rawthey

Baugh Fell

SEDBERGH

Rawthey

TEN MILES

LANCASTER Lune

The Lune starts its life by flowing north-north-east and ends it by flowing south-west into Morecambe Bay at Lancaster. During the course of the journey it drains two sides of the Howgills and a tributary, the Rawthey, almost completes the circuit on the third side of the triangle.

From Green Bell the watershed runs east and south-east to Wild Boar Fell, then south to become contiguous with the Ure Catchment at the head of Garsdale and Wensleydale.

Eden

NEWBIGGIN-ON-LUNE

Lune

RAVENSTONEDALE

Dale Gill

Wyegarth Gill

Scandal Beck

GREEN BELL

Eden Catchment

Lune Catchment

WILD BOAR FELL

Mallerstang

Eden

FIVE MILES

Lune

Rawthey

Ure Catchment

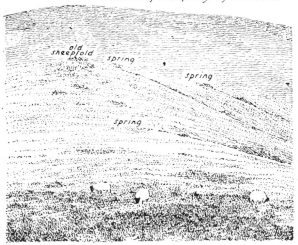

Green Bell from Knoutberry,
   indicating the springs of the Lune

old
sheepfold
   spring

spring

spring

The highest spring

It might reasonably be expected that the proud and patriotic burgesses of Lancaster would have worn a distinct path to the birthplace of their river by frequent pilgrimages. Such is not the case. There is no evidence on the spot that man has ever been there except for a tumbledown sheepfold nearby, built centuries ago. Not only is there no path: there is not even a crushed blade of grass to tell of a passing boot. Obviously the proud and patriotic burgesses of Lancaster have other objectives in their minds.

A beautiful walk on a
fine day; good views and
lovely valley scenery.

Handley's Bridge is identified by its
gate, marked 'Narthwaite'. Cross it
and use the lane from it (note the
old limekiln on the right) until, after
150 yards, it turns sharp left. Here
enter the field on the right (gate),
crossing it by a path to the ford
at Wandale Beck, which cross if you
can and ascend through untidy
scrubland ('Park' is too good a name
for it) to an open pasture, keeping
alongside a wall to Murthwaite.
Turn left here, past a barn, and
incline right to join a good track,
crossing a water cut diverted from Odd Gill. Keep on
this track (which goes towards Adamthwaite) but leave it
in favour of a green path branching off uphill to the
right after half a mile. This path ascends to
a wide desolate hollow from which the top
of Harter Fell is easily attained (no cairn).
Descend northwest over Little Harter Fell
to the tarmac road serving Adamthwaite
from Ravenstonedale, and turn left down
this road until a distinct green path branches
off to the right above a larch plantation.
Beyond a gate in a crosswall this path becomes
indistinct but keep on past a barn to another gate
(difficult to negotiate) in the wall on the left, where
streams join. Now, free of obstacles, traverse
Wandale Hill (no cairn; pool on the summit) and
descend the easy south ridge, joining the Mountain
View path for Narthwaite, where a narrow motor road
slants down amongst fine trees to Handley's Bridge

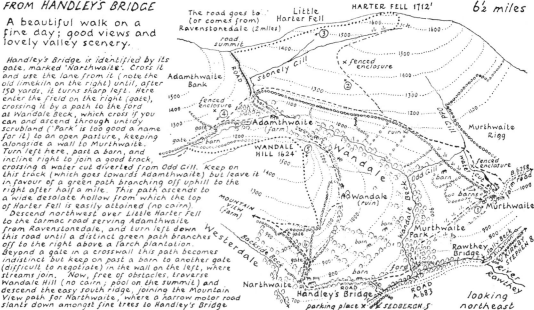

The road goes to
(or comes from)
Ravenstonedale (2 miles)
road summit

Little
Harter Fell

HARTER FELL 1712'

Adamthwaite
Bank

Stonely Gill

× fenced
enclosure

Odd Gill

Murthwaite
Rigg

fenced
enclosure

Adamthwaite
(farm)

gate

barn

ruin

fenced
enclosure

WANDALE
HILL 1624'

Wandale

B.6259

barn

barns

Murthwaite

MOUNTAIN
VIEW
(farm)

Wandale
(ruin)

Wandale Beck

Odd Gill

barns

Murthwaite
Park

Westerdale

Backside Beck

gate

barn

Rawthey
Bridge

KIRKBY
STEPHEN 8

ford

Narthwaite

Handley's Bridge
A.683

River
Rawthey

looking
northeast

parking place × × SEDBERGH 5

MAP

20
(2)

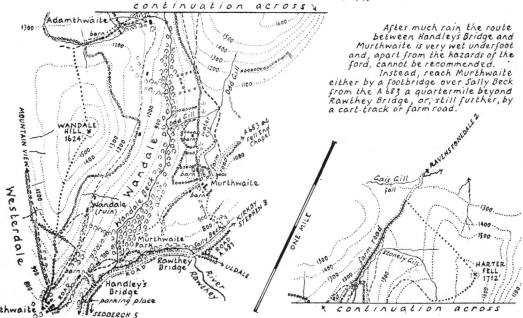

After much rain the route between Handley's Bridge and Murthwaite is very wet underfoot and, apart from the hazards of the ford, cannot be recommended.
  Instead, reach Murthwaite either by a footbridge over Sally Beck from the A 683 a quartermile beyond Rawthey Bridge, or, still further, by a cart-track or farm road.

continuation across

Adamthwaite
barn

MOUNTAIN VIEW

WANDALE HILL ✕ 1624

Wandale Beck

Gill Beck

Odd Gill

A 683 at Fell End Chapel
barn
ford

barn

Murthwaite
barn

Westerdale

Wandale (ruin)

KIRKBY STEPHEN 8

Murthwaite Park
barn

Sally Beck
A 683
ROAD
ULDALE

ROAD
Rawthey Bridge
River Rawthey

barn
Handley's Bridge ← parking place

Narthwaite

SEDBERGH 5

ONE MILE

Gais Gill fall
RAVENSTONEDALE 2

farm road

Stoney Gill
1300
1400
1500

HARTER FELL 1712

continuation across

Murthwaite

Ruined and deserted farmsteads in the valleys
and on the lower slopes of the Howgills — tragic
skeletons that once breathed life —— are all too
commonplace..... Murthwaite occupies a sunny
open position above the trees of Rawthey Bridge
and was formerly a large farming community, but
there is no longer a future for many of these hill
farms and the last residents moved out some years
ago. A neighbour runs his stock on the land, but
they pasture amongst ruins. It is especially sad
to witness death when there is no decent burial.

Adamthwaite

There are many attractively-situated farmhouses
in the side valleys of the Howgills, none more so than
Adamthwaite, deep set amongst lovely trees and in
scenery reminiscent of a Scottish glen. It is remote,
unsuspected and rarely seen.

Although the position of Adamthwaite is south
of the watershed, all its streams draining into the
Rawthey, it is served by road only from the north —
'over the hill' from Ravenstonedale. The telephone
line accompanies this road, but electricity is brought
across the hillside from Fell End.

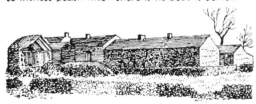

Handley's Bridge

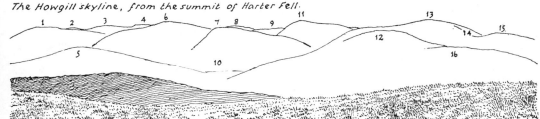

The Howgill skyline, from the summit of Harter Fell.

1 : Great Dummacks
2 : Calders
3 : Bram Rigg Top
4 : The Calf
5 : Wandale Hill
6 : Yarlside
7 : Kensgriff
8 : Wind Scarth
9 : Hazelgill Knott
10 : Westerdale
11 : Randygill Top
12 : Grere Fell
13 : Green Bell
14 : Source of the Lune
15 : Knoutberry
16 : Adamthwaite Bank

—but the most interesting feature of the view is the limestone formation of the Clouds, on the lower slopes of Wild Boar Fell, eastwards, seen as from an aeroplane.

Randygill Top, from the summit of Wandale Hill

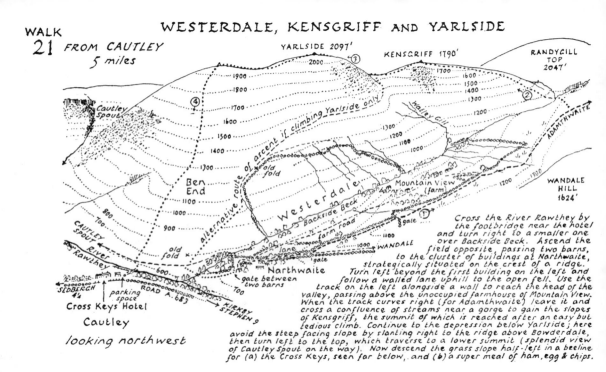

WESTERDALE, KENSGRIFF AND YARLSIDE

YARLSIDE 2097'

KENSGRIFF 1790'

RANDYGILL TOP 2047'

Cautley Spout

alternative route of ascent if climbing Yarlside only

Ben End

Westerdale

Mountain View (farm)

Backside Beck

Waley Gill

WANDALE HILL 1624'

ADAMTHWAITE

old fold

farm road

gate

CAUTLEY SPOUT

River Rawthey

old fold

Narthwaite

lane

gate

WANDALE

gate between two barns

SEDBERGH 4¼

parking space

Cross Keys Hotel

Cautley

ROAD A.683

KIRKBY STEPHEN 9

looking northwest

Cross the River Rawthey by the footbridge near the hotel and turn right to a smaller one over Backside Beck. Ascend the field opposite, passing two barns, to the cluster of buildings at Narthwaite, strategically situated on the crest of a ridge. Turn left beyond the first building on the left and follow a walled lane uphill to the open fell. Use the track on the left alongside a wall to reach the head of the valley, passing above the unoccupied farmhouse of Mountain View. When the track curves right (for Adamthwaite) leave it and cross a confluence of streams near a gorge to gain the slopes of Kensgriff, the summit of which is reached after an easy but tedious climb. Continue to the depression below Yarlside; here avoid the steep facing slope by slanting right to the ridge above Bowderdale, then turn left to the top, which traverse to a lower summit (splendid view of Cautley Spout on the way). Now descend the grass slope half-left in a beeline for (a) the Cross Keys, seen far below, and (b) a super meal of ham, egg & chips.

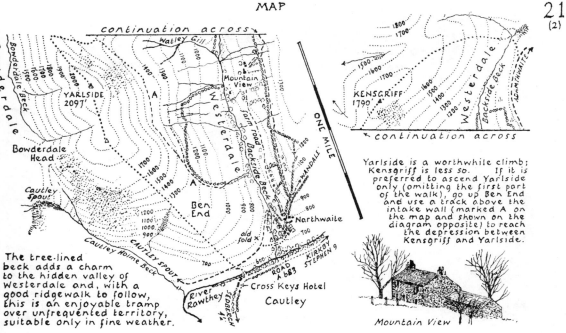

MAP

21
(2)

continuation across

Watley Gill

Mountain View

YARLSIDE
2097'

Bowderdale Beck

W e s t e r d a l e

Bowderdale

A

farm road

Backside Beck

Bowderdale
Head

A

WANDALE

Ben
End

Narthwaite

Cautley
Spout

old
fold ×

CAUTLEY SPOUT

Cautley Holme Beck

ONE MILE

KENSGRIFF
1790'

W e s t e r d a l e

Backside Beck

RAWTHWAITE

continuation across

Yarlside is a worthwhile climb;
Kensgriff is less so. If it is
preferred to ascend Yarlside
only (omitting the first part
of the walk), go up Ben End
and use a track above the
intake wall (marked A on
the map and shown on the
diagram opposite) to reach
the depression between
Kensgriff and Yarlside.

The tree-lined
beck adds a charm
to the hidden valley of
Westerdale and, with a
good ridgewalk to follow,
this is an enjoyable tramp
over unfrequented territory,
suitable only in fine weather.

ROAD A 683

KIRKBY
STEPHEN 9

FEDRAUGH

River
Rawthey

Cross Keys Hotel
Cautley

Mountain View

Narthwaite

Cross Keys Hotel
Cautley

HAM
AND
EGGS

Gorge at the head of
Westerdale

Kensgriff: the Westerdale flank

The summit of Kensgriff
looking east across Westerdale to Wandale Hill, with
Wild Boar Fell and Swarth Fell in the background.

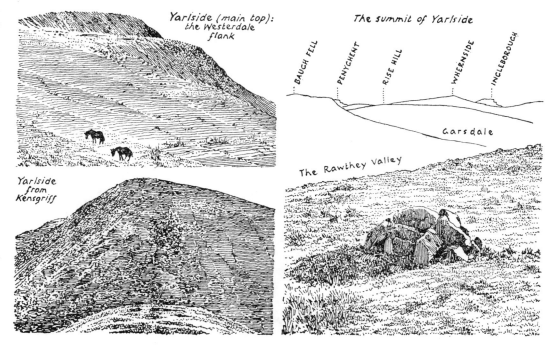

Yarlside (main top): the Westerdale flank

The summit of Yarlside

BAUGH FELL PENYGHENT RISE HILL WHERNSIDE INGLEBOROUGH

Garsdale

The Rawthey Valley

Yarlside from Kensgriff

The view from Yarlside

The slightly higher ground of the Calf plateau restricts the view southwest but in all other directions the panorama is very extensive, ranging from the Lakeland fells, seen as an uninterrupted skyline from the Coniston group to Carrock Fell with the Scafells and Great Gable and Helvellyn prominent, to Cross Fell and the Pennines; the nearer ridge of Wild Boar Fell, Swarth Fell and Baugh Fell framing a glimpse of the Wensleydale hills; and, unmistakable, the three limestone giants of Penyghent, Whernside and Ingleborough. On the descent to the lower summit Cautley Spout comes fully into view, presenting a scene not excelled by any other series of waterfalls in the country.

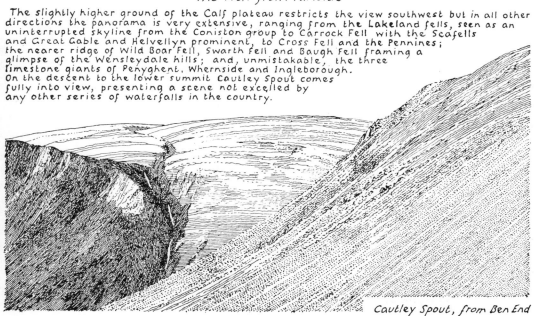

Cautley Spout, from Ben End

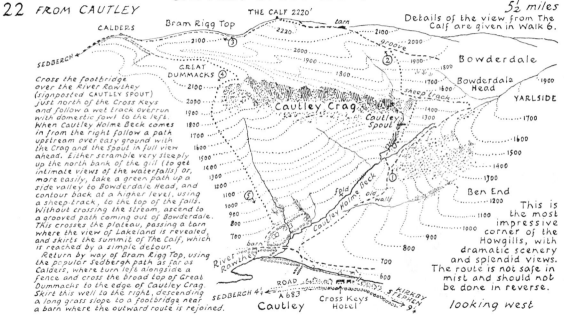

WALK 22 FROM CAUTLEY

CAUTLEY SPOUT AND THE CALF

5½ miles

Details of the view from The Calf are given in Walk 6.

THE CALF 2220'

Bram Rigg Top

CALDERS

SEDBERGH

tarn

groove

Bowderdale

Bowderdale Head

YARLSIDE

GREAT DUMMACKS

Cautley Crag

Cautley Spout

sheep-track

Cross the footbridge over the River Rawthey (signposted CAUTLEY SPOUT) just north of the Cross Keys and follow a wet track overrun with domestic fowl to the left. When Cautley Holme Beck comes in from the right follow a path upstream over easy ground with the Crag and the spout in full view ahead. Either scramble very steeply up the north bank of the gill (to get intimate views of the waterfalls) or, more easily, take a green path up a side valley to Bowderdale Head, and contour back at a higher level, using a sheep-track, to the top of the falls. Without crossing the stream, ascend to a grooved path coming out of Bowderdale. This crosses the plateau, passing a tarn where the view of Lakeland is revealed, and skirts the summit of The Calf, which is reached by a simple detour.

Return by way of Bram Rigg Top, using the popular Sedbergh path as far as Calders, where turn left alongside a fence and cross the broad top of Great Dummacks to the edge of Cautley Crag. Skirt this well to the right, descending a long grass slope to a footbridge near a barn where the outward route is rejoined.

Cautley Holme Beck

old walls

Ben End

This is the most impressive corner of the Howgills, with dramatic scenery and splendid views. The route is not safe in mist and should not be done in reverse.

looking west

River Rawthey

barn

ROAD

SEDBERGH 4½ ← A 683

Cautley

Cross Keys Hotel

KIRKBY STEPHEN 9½

MAP

22
(2)

Cautley Crag is a cliff almost a mile in length formed by a series of steep buttresses that are too broken and friable to provide any serious rockclimbing. It is the only extensive mass of exposed rock on the Howgill Fells.

Cautley Spout is really a succession of waterfalls in a vertical height of 700 feet but the name is usually reserved for the main fall, the finest in the Howgills and one of the highest in the country.

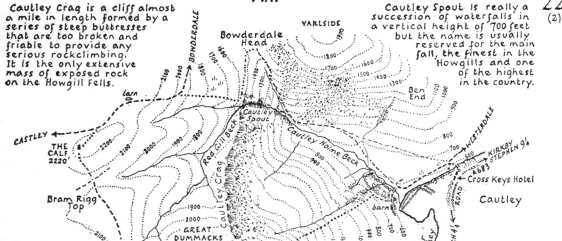

ONE MILE

The main fall

The upper falls

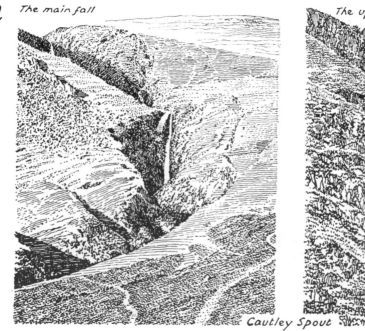

Cautley Spout

WALK
23

FROM CAUTLEY
A long and tedious ascent; a supreme
moment; and a charming valley.

5 miles

*There is usually space to park a car by the roadside
opposite the lane to Steps End. Walk down this lane,
bearing right past the farmhouse to a footbridge behind.
Across this, go up an overgrown lane, which turns right
to join an old track above the intake fence. Keep right
along it for 120 yards, then, beyond a stream-crossing,
take a rising green drove-road branching to the left.
When this peters out swing left at an easy gradient
to gain the south ridge of Great Dummacks and
follow it up to the summit — a mile-long easy
ascent on featureless grass and bilberry. The
moment of arrival at the edge of Cautley Crag,
with a vast abyss suddenly at one's feet and
surprising new views ahead, is worth all the
effort. Cross the flat peaty top of Great
Dummacks, aiming for the cairn on Calders,
but turn left down by the wire fence on
Middle Tongue. (Ingleborough is visible
directly ahead). When the fence goes off
to the right keep straight down the
ridge to the confluence of Hobdale Gill
and Grimes Gill, crossing the latter to
join a track above the left bank of
the combined waters, now known as
Hobdale Beck. Pass through a gate
in a wall to descend alongside a
wooded ravine to Fawcett Bank.
From the farm take the
higher track, neglected
and overgrown, for half a mile,
when a gate on the right
gives access to the
footbridge at Steps
End.*

looking north-west

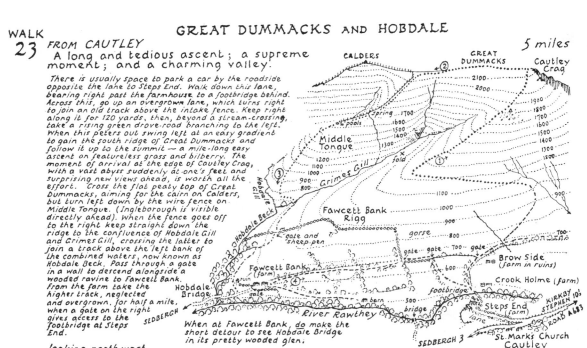

*When at Fawcett Bank, do make the
short detour to see Hobdale Bridge
in its pretty wooded glen.*

MAP

23
(2)

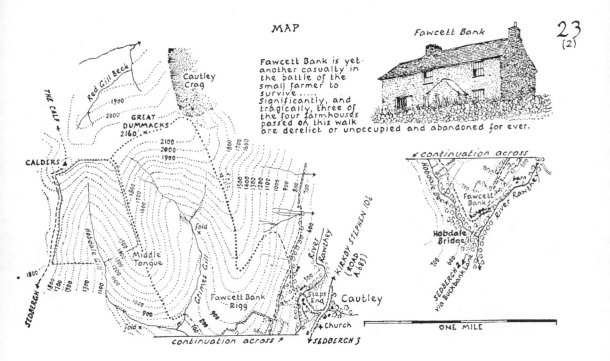

Fawcett Bank

Fawcett Bank is yet
another casualty in
the battle of the
small farmer to
survive.....
Significantly, and
tragically, three of
the four farmhouses
passed on this walk
are derelict or unoccupied and abandoned for ever.

ONE MILE

Cautley Crag

The drawing shows the scene looking down the cliffs to the ravine of Cautley Spout. In the distance is Bowderdale, flanked by Hazelgill Knott on the left and West Fell beyond, and on the right by Randygill Top and Yarlside.

This is the most impressive view in the Howgills, and all the more dramatic because it bursts suddenly upon the eye with the force of a blow after the uninteresting climb up the south ridge.

The view from Great Dummacks

The summit is flat, and, in the absence of a cairn, it is difficult to determine the highest point. Much of Lakeland is concealed by the plateau, only two sections being visible — the Coniston fells and the skyline from Great Gable to Helvellyn. But in other directions the panorama is extensive, the principal heights being Cross Fell and Mickle Fell far away in the north, the nearby Wild Boar Fell eastwards, and Baugh Fell, Whernside and Ingleborough further round to the south.

left: *Hobdale — looking up the valley to Middle Tongue, with Calders forming the left skyline and Great Dummacks the right.*

below: *Hobdale Bridge*

SICKERS FELL AND KNOTT

FROM SEDBERGH

4½ miles

From the main street turn up Joss Lane (between the Congregational Church and a public car park) to its end at a gate with Hill Farm ahead. Incline left to a wooded dell and ascend it to a kissing gate in the intake wall. Go down to the beck, cross it above the waterfall and climb the opposite bank to the top corner of the wall. From this point follow a rising green path due east (it is, in fact, a pipe track), traversing the breast of Crook and turning north into Ashbeck Gill to a small dam and recording hut of the Water Board. Cross the dam and ascend the facing slope to the top of Sickers Fell, thence making a beeline for Knott and returning to Ashbeck Gill alongside the intake wall. Cross the beck and follow the wall below Crook to an awkward stile that gives access to the rifle range used by Sedbergh School. Go down this field to a stile and alongside a fence to a cart track leading down to Thorns Lane and the A.683.

A simple half-day expedition; easy walking and fine views.

looking north-north-east

The notice boards warn of the perils of proceeding when the rifle range is in use.

Knott is a cornerstone of the Howgills and has excellent aerial views of the Rawthey valley and Garsdale.

Summit cairn Sickers Fell

Summit cairn Knott

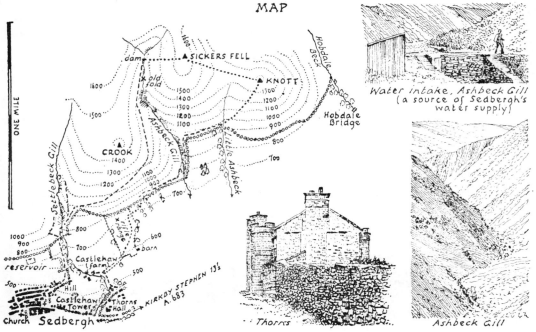

MAP

24
(2)

Water intake, Ashbeck Gill
(a source of Sedbergh's
water supply)

ONE MILE

dam ▲ SICKERS FELL

old
fold ▲ KNOTT

Hobdale Beck

1600

1500

CROOK
1400

1300

1200

Ashbeck Gill

1500
1400
1300
1200
1100

1300
1200
1100
1000
900
800
700

Hobdale Bridge

Little Ashbeck

Settlebeck Gill

1000
900
800

800

700

barn

600

1000
900
800
reservoir

Castlehaw
(farm)

500

Hill
Castlehaw
Tower

Thorns
Hall

KIRKBY STEPHEN 13½
A.683

Church Sedbergh

Thorns

Ashbeck Gill

From the main street turn up Joss Lane (between the Congregational Church and a public car park) to its end at a gate with Hill Farm ahead. Incline left to a pleasant wooded dell and ascend it, using stiles, to a kissing gate in the intake wall. The main path turns left uphill, but go down to the beck, crossing it above the waterfall. Crook can now be climbed straight up, but it is preferable, at the wall corner, to follow a rising green path in the bracken that runs across the breast of the fell and turns into the deep valley of Ashbeck Gill. Watch for a grooved path on the left, near boulders: this leads up onto the ridge with the double summit of Crook nearby on the left.

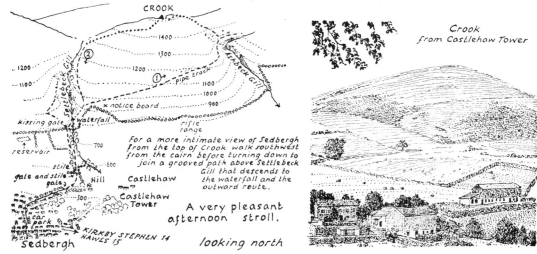

CROOK

1400
1300
1200
1100
②
pipe track
①
1100
1000
900
× notice board
1200
kissing gate   waterfall
rifle range
reservoir
700
stile
600
gate and stile
gate   Hill   Castlehaw
500
Castlehaw Tower
car park
KIRKBY STEPHEN 14
HAWES 15
Sedbergh

Settlebeck Gill
Ashbeck Gill

For a more intimate view of Sedbergh from the top of Crook walk southwest from the cairn before turning down to join a grooved path above Settlebeck Gill that descends to the waterfall and the outward route.

A very pleasant afternoon stroll.

looking north

Crook from Castlehow Tower

MAP

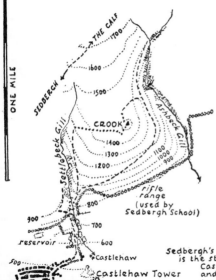

ONE MILE

THE CALF

1700

1600

1500

SEDBERGH

CROOK

1400

1300

1200

1100 1000 900

Settlebeck Gill

Ashbeck Gill

rifle range (used by Sedbergh School)

800

900

700

reservoir

600

500

castlehaw

Castlehaw Tower

car park

Church Sedbergh

KIRKBY STEPHEN 14
HAWES 15

Summit cairn on Crook

Surprisingly, the unimportant summit of Crook has the largest cairn of all.

Settlebeck Gill

The waters of Settlebeck Gill, augmented from Ashbeck Gill, are a principal source of Sedbergh's water supply. The rising path around Crook to Ashbeck Gill is really a pipeline track

Sedbergh's most notable antiquity is the steep artificial mound of Castlehaw Tower, a 'motte and bailey castle.' There is some doubt about its origin and excavations have failed to reveal traces of occupation.

PART THREE

THE MALLERSTANG-GARSDALE-RAWTHEY TRIANGLE

THE MALLERSTANG—GARSDALE—RAWTHEY TRIANGLE

INTRODUCTION

The territory described in this part of the book is less compact than the adjoining Howgill Fells but equally well defined, forming a single wedge of high ground rising from a surround of deep valleys. The shape of the area is similarly triangular, but in this case the base is to the south and the apex is north. Quite unlike the Howgills, which form a cluster of summits above steep slopes, here there are three 'tops' only in an area of roughly the same size and they surmount sprawling slopes of gentler inclination, the character of the terrain being much more Pennine. The underlying rocks, too, are different : caps of millstone grit on layers of sandstone and shale with a pronounced limestone belt along the west.

The three main fells are Wild Boar Fell, Swarth Fell and Baugh Fell. The first two are bounded by the valley of Mallerstang in the east. Baugh Fell, a moorland of great girth, extends the full length of Garsdale in the south and of the Rawthey valley in the west. The northern part of the western boundary is a limestone trough not defined by a watercourse. Of the rain that falls on the area the Lune collects most through the agency of the rivers Rawthey and Clough, but the precipitation on the eastern fringe finds its way into the Eden and, in smaller degree, into the Ure. The Eden also benefits from northern feeders. The Westmorland-Yorkshire county boundary divides the area with a bias in favour of Yorkshire.

These hills too are very lonely. Wild Boar Fell is a commanding height with an appeal to walkers, Swarth Fell is virtually unknown and Baugh Fell is an upland wilderness rarely visited. Nevertheless they have attractions in plenty and in wide variety, and hidden beauties revealed only to those who search for them on foot — as the following pages will tell.

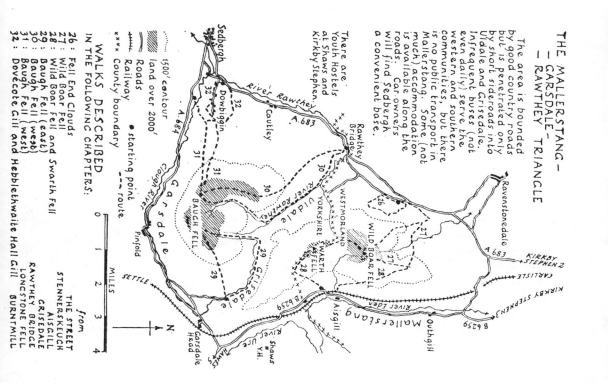

THE MALLERSTANG –
– GARSDALE –
– RAWTHEY TRIANGLE

The area is bounded by good country roads but is penetrated only by short sideroads into Uldale and Grisedale. Infrequent buses (not even daily) serve the western and southern communities, but there is no public transport in Mallerstang. Some (not much) accommodation is available along the roads. Car-owners will find Sedbergh a convenient base.

There are Youth Hostels at Shaws and Kirkby Stephen.

·········· 1500' contour
▨▨▨▨ land over 2000'
╪╪╪╪ Roads
┼┼┼┼ Railway
×××× County boundary
● starting point
-- -- route

WALKS DESCRIBED IN THE FOLLOWING CHAPTERS:

26 : Fell End Clouds
27 : Wild Boar Fell
28 : Wild Boar Fell and Swarth Fell
29 : Baugh Fell (east)
30 : Baugh Fell (west)
31 : Baugh Fell (west)
32 : Dovecote Gill and Hebblethwaite Hall Gill

from
THE STREET
STENNERSKEUGH
CRISEDALE
AISGILL
RAWTHEY BRIDGE
LONGSTONE FELL
BURNTMILL

MILES
0 1 2 3 4

N

FELL END CLOUDS

3 miles

The old road is still
often referred to by its
former name: *The Street*

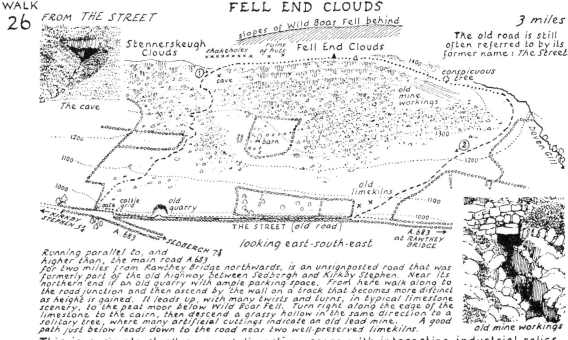

slopes of Wild Boar Fell behind

Stennerskeugh
Clouds

shakeholes   ruins
of huts

Fell End Clouds

1400

conspicuous
tree

① cave

old
mine
workings

The cave

1200

1300

②

1100

barn

1200

1000

old
limekilns

1100

cattle
grid

old quarry

1000

KIRKBY
STEPHEN 5½

A.683

SEDBERGH 7¼

THE STREET (old road)

A.683 →
at RAWTHEY
BRIDGE

looking east-south-east

Doven Gill

Running parallel to, and
higher than, the main road A683
for two miles from Rawthey Bridge northwards, is an unsignposted road that was
formerly part of the old highway between Sedbergh and Kirkby Stephen. Near its
northern end is an old quarry with ample parking space. From here walk along to
the road junction and then ascend by the wall on a track that becomes more distinct
as height is gained. It leads up, with many twists and turns, in typical limestone
scenery, to the peat moor below Wild Boar Fell. Turn right along the edge of the
limestone to the cairn, then descend a grassy hollow in the same direction to a
solitary tree, where many artificial cuttings indicate an old lead mine.   A good
path just below leads down to the road near two well-preserved limekilns.

old mine workings

This is a simple stroll amongst limestone scars with interesting industrial relics.

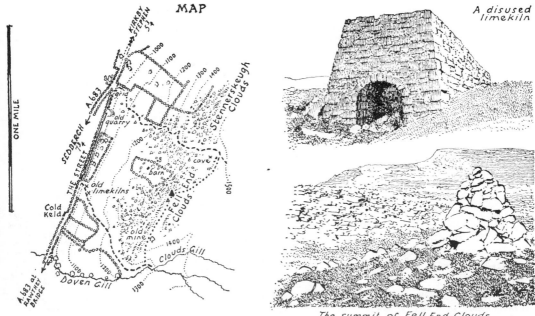

MAP

ONE MILE

A disused limekiln

The summit of Fell End Clouds,
looking to Stennerskeugh Clouds.

WALK
27 FROM STENNERSKEUGH

WILD BOAR FELL
2324'

7 miles

This is the least interesting side of
Wild Boar Fell but the walk thereto
and therefrom is pleasant.

The Nab

2200
2100
2000
1900
1800

Sand Tarn

Millstones were made
on the boulder slopes
above Sand Tarn. Some
may still be found by
diligent search.

Little Fell
1831'

gate

Greenrigg Moss

Low Greenrigg

1700
1600
1500

Scandal Beck

old fold

1800

1600

1500

looking south-east

1300

1400

Hasky Gill

1409

old fold

Turn off the A.683 alongside a wall to Street
Farm and continue forward (on the line of the
old road used before the A 683 was made) to
Clouds Lane, noting on the right as this fork
is approached the handsome gateway and the
castellated walls of a mansion that formerly
occupied the wooded grounds over the wall. At
the top of Clouds Lane, on the open fell, take
the second track on the right (the first is used
when returning): this deteriorates as Scandal
Beck is approached. Ford the stream to a gate
in the opposite wall, which is succeeded at once

1300

Scandal Beck

x old mine

1300

1500

ruin

old limekiln

Stennerskeugh
Clouds

1200

High
Stennerskeugh
(farm)

gate

1100

Stennerskeugh
(farm)

Clouds

1000

by a gate in a new fence. From here to the ridge ahead it is difficult to
trace the path (a bridleway over to Mallerstang), but aim well to the right
of the dip in the skyline, gaining the ridge at a wicket gate in the corner of
the wall running up to and along it. Now turn right along the edge of an
impressive escarpment, ascending more steeply to the Nab (best spot
for a rest and an appraisal of the views). Cross the level top to the
obvious summit of the fell (O.S. column No 10797). The descent
may be made in a beeline for Stennerskeugh,
keeping to the right of the broad plateau of
Greenrigg Moss to avoid wet ground.
A fair track will be found near an old
sheepfold and this leads down easily
to the top of Clouds Lane.

Street

Street
Farm

KIRKBY
STEPHEN 5¼

A 683

cattle
grid

old
quarry

site of
toll bar

SEDBERGH 7¾

There are many unofficial
parking places on the unenclosed A 683
but the old quarry on the side road is
the most spacious and the walk is
deemed to start from this point.

MAP

27
(2)

Stennerskeugh

Street

High
Stennerskeugh

Street Farm

hen hut

barn

grid

old
quarry

Stennerskeugh
Clouds

ruin

x old limekiln

old
mine

High Stennerskeugh
and the old limekiln

Long Gill

Scandal Beck

Hasty Gill

old
fold

x old fold

MALLERSTANG

Low
Greenrigg

Greenrigg
Moss

The Nab

Sand Tarn

WILD BOAR FELL
2324'

SEDBERGH

A683 at
Rawthey
Bridge

KIRKBY STEPHEN

Clouds Lane

ONE MILE

Wild Boar Fell is reputed to be
the place where the last wild boar
in England was shot. It is the
highest of the fells described in
this book and is prominently in
view from the valley of the Eden,
of which most of its streams are
feeders. Geologically it is interesting,
sandstone and shale lying on a bed of
mountain limestone under a cap of
millstone grit. Lead has been mined,
stone quarried, lime burned and peat cut
on its western flanks, millstones have been
fashioned from its summit boulders and
no doubt scythes have been sharpened
on the gritty beaches of Sand Tarn. But
today it is untouched by industry and is free range for
sheep and ponies and a few discerning human walkers.

The
north
ridge

The small mound on the top of
the Nab, occupied by a cairn,
is a tumulus.
The altitude
here is 2296'.

The Nab

The summit is a slight swelling of the wide plateau. A triangulation column of the Ordnance Survey fits snugly into a wind-shelter.

As a viewpoint it is inferior to the Nab, which has the advantage of a sharp declivity to reveal valley details: the view from the summit itself, although slightly more extensive, is robbed of detail by the broad expanses of grass all around. From the Nab there is a far prospect of the Eden valley backed by Cross Fell, with Kirkby Stephen prominent; the upper valley of the Lune is also seen, and Mallerstang is directly below. Great Shunner Fell and Lovely Seat appear over Abbotside Common eastwards; to the south, Ingleborough and Whernside are framed by the nearer Widdale Fell and Swarth Fell, while to the west is the long skyline of the Howgills with many of the Lakeland giants on the far horizon. The views are enhanced and given dramatic effect by the escarpment.

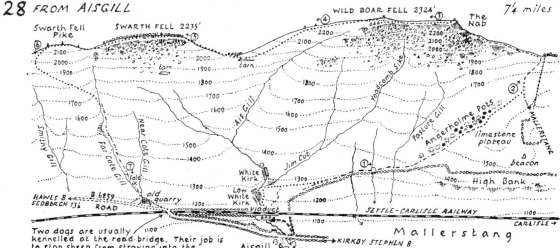

Swarth Fell Pike

SWARTH FELL 2235'

WILD BOAR FELL 2324'

The Nab

⑥ 2100
2000
1900

⑤

2100
2000
tarn
1900
1800
1700
1600

④ 2200
2100
tarn
1800
1700
1600
1500

③ 2200
2100
1900
1800
1700

②

Smithy Gill

1700
1600

Far Cote Gill
Near Cote Gill

Ais Gill

1500
1400

1300

old quarry

fold

⑦
1400

1300

White Kirk

Low White Kirk

Jim Cut

1300

Yoadcomb Sike

Pasture Gill

Angerholme Pots

limestone plateau

① 1400
1300

beacon

High Bank

MALLERSTANG

HAWES 8
SEDBERGH 13½
B 6259
ROAD
1100

Viaduct

1200

1200

SETTLE–CARLISLE RAILWAY

1100

CARLISLE →

Aisgill
(farm)

→ KIRKBY STEPHEN 8

River Eden

M a l l e r s t a n g

Two dogs are usually kennelled at the road-bridge. Their job is to stop sheep from straying into the enclosed road from the open fell — a sort of canine cattle grid.

This bridge is an excellent 'station' for railway enthusiasts with cameras. Wild Boar Fell makes an imposing background as trains come round the curve on the long climb out of Mallerstang to Aisgill Summit.

looking west

More than any other in the book, this expedition savours of real mountaineering, the ramparts forming an exciting parade. A little elementary potholing is included for good measure.

An old quarry by the roadside near the railway bridge is the best place to leave a car. From here go down the road until opposite Aisgill Farm, where an uphill track on the left passes under the railway viaduct to the limestone ravine of Ais Gill, a habitat of interesting plants and mosses and a place of exciting waterfalls and grottoes seen only by a rough passage up the stony bed of the stream. There is no time for a detailed exploration today, however. Bear to the right across the moor to accompany the intake wall until it turns away towards the valley. Now aim for the ridge at the end of the escarpment of Wild Boar Fell, bearing slightly left to follow the obvious fracture between the peaty moor and the limestone pavements and passing a score or more of shakeholes and potholes, some of which are quite dangerous. Beyond this area a slanting path leads up to the ridge, where turn left along the crest of the escarpment to the Nab, which has a fine aerial view of the ground so far covered. Visit the next 'headland', where there are six cairns and unlimited supplies of stones for making more, before crossing the flat top of the fell to the summit (O.S. column Nº 10797). Aim southwest inclining south down to the depression between Wild Boar Fell and Swarth Fell: keep left to avoid peat-hags. A wall coming up from Uldale and marking the county boundary is joined here. There is no difficulty in crossing Swarth Fell, which has its own escarpment, and Swarth Fell Pike, which has two fine shepherds' cairns and a good view forward of the hidden valley of Grisedale. Now turn down left to the road across an easy moor, guided by Far Cote Gill, which spills into the quarry where the car is parked.

Aisgill Farm

Ais Gill:
White Kirk

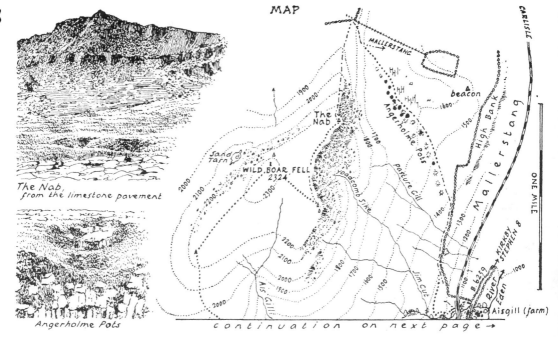

MAP

The Nab,
from the limestone pavement

Angerholme Pots

CARLISLE

MALLERSTANG

beacon

High Bank

Mallerstang

ONE MILE

The Nab

Angerholme Pots

1900
2000
Sand Tarn
WILD BOAR FELL
2324
2000
2100
2200

Yoadcomb Sike

Pasture Gill

1800
1700
1600
1400
1300
1200
1100
1000

2100
2000
1900
1800
1700
1600
1500

Ais Gill

Jim Cut

B 6259

River Eden

KIRKBY STEPHEN 8

Aisgill (farm)

c o n t i n u a t i o n   o n   n e x t   p a g e →

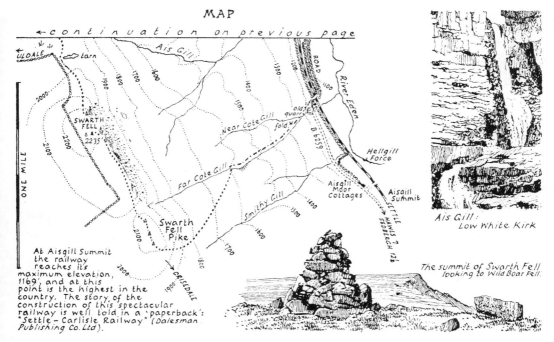

MAP

← c o n t i n u a t i o n   o n   p r e v i o u s   p a g e

28
(4)

ULDALE
tarn
Ais Gill
ROAD
River Eden

2000
2100
2200
1900
1800
1700
1600
1300
1200
1100

SWARTH
FELL
△ A.
2235

ONE MILE

Near Cote Gill
fold
old
quarry
B 6259

2100

Far Cote Gill

Swarth
Fell
Pike

Smithy Gill

Hellgill
Force

Aisgill
Moor
Cottages

Aisgill
Summit

SETTLE
HAWES 7
SEDBERGH 12½

1500
1600
1700
1800
1900
2000

GARSDALE

At Aisgill Summit
the railway
reaches its
maximum elevation,
1169', and at this
point is the highest in the
country. The story of the
construction of this spectacular
railway is well told in a 'paperback':
"Settle–Carlisle Railway" (Dalesman
Publishing Co.Ltd).

Ais Gill:
Low White Kirk

The summit of Swarth Fell
looking to Wild Boar Fell.

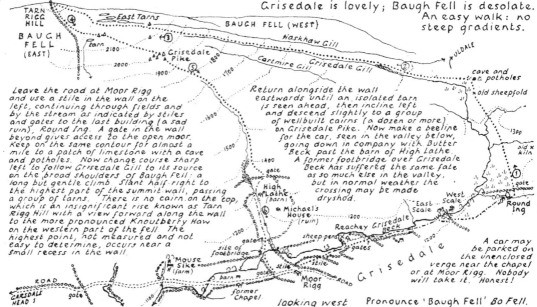

BAUGH FELL (EAST)

6½ miles

Grisedale is lovely; Baugh Fell is desolate.
An easy walk: no
steep gradients.

TARN
RIGG
HILL ④ *East Tarns*
BAUGH FELL (WEST)

BAUGH
FELL
(EAST) *Tarn* 2100 ③ Haskhaw Gill

2000 Grisedale Pike
1800 Cartmire Gill Grisedale Gill
1900 ⑤ 1700 ②

cave and
tarn potholes

old sheepfold

1300

old x
kiln

Leave the road at Moor Rigg
and use a stile in the wall on the
left, continuing through fields and
by the stream as indicated by stiles
and gates to the last building (a sad
ruin), Round Ing. A gate in the wall
beyond gives access to the open moor.
Keep on the same contour for almost a
mile to a patch of limestone with a cave
and potholes. Now change course sharp
left to follow Grisedale Gill to its source
on the broad shoulders of Baugh Fell: a
long but gentle climb. Slant half-right to
the highest part of the summit wall, passing
a group of tarns. There is no cairn on the top,
which is an insignificant rise known as Tarn
Rigg Hill with a view forward along the wall
to the more pronounced Knoutberry Haw
on the western part of the fell. The
highest point, not measured and not
easy to determine, occurs near a
small recess in the wall.

Return alongside the wall
eastwards until an isolated tarn
is seen ahead, then incline left
and descend slightly to a group
of wellbuilt cairns (a dozen or more)
on Grisedale Pike. Now make a beeline
for the car, seen in the valley below,
going down in company with Butter
Beck past the barn of High Lathe.
A former footbridge over Grisedale
Beck has suffered the same fate
as so much else in the valley,
but in normal weather the
crossing may be made
dryshod.

1600
1500
1400
gate
1300
High
Lathe
(barn)
1200
East
Scale
West
Scale
Reachey Grisedale Beck
Round
Ing
site of
footbridge
gates
Michael's
House
(ruin)
sheep pen
gates
1200
gate
1300

Mouse
Sike
(farm)
barn
gates
stile
stile
Moor
Rigg
ROAD

A car may
be parked on
the unenclosed
verge near the chapel
or at Moor Rigg. Nobody
will take it. Honest!

Grisedale

ROAD
GARSDALE
HEAD 1
gate
former
Chapel

looking west   Pronounce 'Baugh Fell' BO Fell.

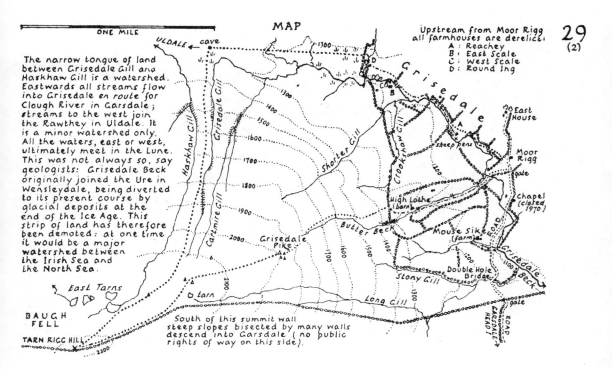

MAP

ONE MILE

ULDALE ← cave

The narrow tongue of land between Grisedale Gill and Haskhaw Gill is a watershed. Eastwards all streams flow into Grisedale en route for Clough River in Garsdale; streams to the west join the Rawthey in Uldale. It is a minor watershed only. All the waters, east or west, ultimately meet in the Lune. This was not always so, say geologists: Grisedale Beck originally joined the Ure in Wensleydale, being diverted to its present course by glacial deposits at the end of the Ice Age. This strip of land has therefore been demoted: at one time it would be a major watershed between the Irish Sea and the North Sea.

Haskhaw Gill

Grisedale Gill

Cartmire Gill

Grisedale

East House

Shorter Gill

Crookhaw Gill

sheep pens

Moor Rigg

gate

High Lathe (barn)

Chapel (closed 1970)

Butler Beck

Mouse Sike (farm)

ROAD

Grisedale Beck

Grisedale Pike

Stony Gill

Double Hole Bridge

Long Gill

ROAD GARSDALE HEAD

gate

ROAD GARSDALE →

East Tarns

tarn

BAUGH FELL

TARN RIGG HILL

2200

1300 1300 1400 1500 1600 1700 1800 1900 2000 1700 1600 1500 1400 1300 1200 1100

South of this summit wall steep slopes bisected by many walls descend into Garsdale (no public rights of way on this side).

'Grisedale' is pronounced *Grizedale* (the valley of the wild swine). Ordnance map-makers spell the name *Grisdale* (without the middle 'e') but are alone in doing so.

Knoutberry Haw
from Tarn Rigg Hill

Wild Boar Fell
and Swarth Fell
from Baugh Fell

Cave at the head of Grisedale

Cairns on Baugh Fell often occur in pairs, forming a 'gateway'. These have been built not by walkers but by shepherds. They are a clue to location in mist and mark ways off the fell; they are not intended, as most cairns are, to indicate summits or viewpoints. They are *working* cairns, not *amenity* cairns.

looking down Wensleydale
from Grisedale Pike

The cairns on Grisedale Pike, at least twelve in number, were erected at some trouble, the hollows nearby apparently being the quarries opened to provide the stones. They have no special significance but it is perhaps no coincidence that, at this point, there is a superb distant view down Wensleydale and one can appreciate here the opinions of the geologists that Grisedale was once an extension of that valley, its waters flowing into the River Ure until deflected to their present course by glacial deposits at Garsdale Head.

Grisedale

Grisedale is an oasis of emerald fields enclosed by dark moors and watered by sparkling streams. On a sunny day in springtime, with the new lambs frisking and the birds singing in ecstasy, the place seems a very heaven, a sanctuary. No traffic. Music but no noise.... Just stillness and peace.

At the turn of the century this pleasant valley was the home of a hardworking and happy farming community. A dozen families lived here, brought up children and worshipped in a tiny chapel.

Today it is a graveyard of ruined farmhouses. Good pastures are turning sour; paths are overgrown..... It has the sadness of death. Hard economic facts have driven life away. Only one farmer still calls it home, but happily others from outside use some of the pastures as grazing, else all would revert to wilderness. The chapel, its congregation reduced to an average of three, has closed its doors for ever. Even God has been driven out.

Few people know Grisedale. It is an upland valley, a hollow of the fells above Garsdale, out of sight and completely unsuspected by travellers on the A.684. A wide band of heather moor crosses its portals; the green fields beyond, over a thousand feet up, are a great surprise.

Bridge at East Scale

The ruins of Round Ing

Has it a future? As grazing land, yes; but most of the homesteads are decayed beyond redemption. Were it better known, these dwellings might have been saved and restored, but the present clamour for country retreats has come too late to restore Grisedale. The Forestry Commission are moving in. And where the beck plunges down a narrow ravine into Garsdale a small dam could impound a large reservoir; an ominous rain-gauge has already been installed. But surely not. Abandoned it may be, but Grisedale is too beautiful to be drowned. There are too few Grisedales left to delight the eye and offer safe haven to birds and animals and so many wild flowers that flourish best in solitude.

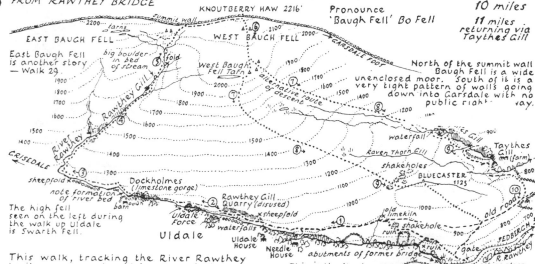

KNOUTBERRY HAW 2216'

Pronounce 'Baugh Fell' Bo Fell

10 miles

11 miles returning via Taythes Gill

EAST BAUGH FELL

WEST BAUGH FELL

East Baugh Fell is another story — Walk 29.

big boulder in bed of stream

fold

West Baugh Fell Tarn

alternative route of descent

North of the summit wall Baugh Fell is a wide unenclosed moor. South of it is a very tight pattern of walls going down into Garsdale with no public right of way.

GARSDALE FOOT

Rawthey Gill

River Rawthey

GRISEDALE

waterfall

Taythes Gill

Raven Thorn Gill

Taythes Gill (farm)

shakeholes

BLUECASTER 1125

sheepfold

Dockholmes (limestone gorge)

Rawthey Gill Quarry (disused)

note formation of river bed

The high fell seen on the left during the walk up Uldale is Swarth Fell.

barn

Uldale Force

waterfalls

Uldale

Uldale House

Needle House

abutments of former bridge

old limekiln

shakehole

ruin

ruin

old road

gate

SEDBERGH 5

R. Rawthey

parking place

This is the 'top' road (the old road, formerly known as 'the Street'). It rejoins the A 683 after two miles and has a branch to Uldale.

Rawthey Bridge

A 683 KIRKBY STEPHEN 8

looking south

This walk, tracking the River Rawthey to its source, should be regarded as a major expedition requiring a full day. The river is a delightful companion, but Baugh Fell is a vast wilderness. Fine, clear weather is essential, not for safety but for enjoyment.

A commodious parking place near Rawthey Bridge is the starting point (and, it is hoped, the finishing point). Cross the roadside fence opposite (gate 50 yards down) and contour along the side of Bluecaster, ignoring a grooved path (the old road) turning up to the right. A track soon appears and passes above a first walled enclosure and then another, each with a ruined barn. Beyond the second, bear right by a big shakehole to join a distinct path at a higher level. This goes forward into mid-Uldale, descending to the riverside at a wooden bridge (which do not cross). The next mile upriver is delightful. A thin track (an overgrown quarry road) continues past a succession of waterfalls to a quarried cliff. Beyond this, climb the slope on the right to avoid the impasse of Uldale Force, seen ahead, and continue above the ravine on a helpful sheeptrack. (Photographers, note that the Force is difficult and dangerous to approach closely). Now the view ahead is more open. The long limestone gorge of Dockholmes is next reached and, if entered along the side of the river, also necessitates an escape on the right to circumvent cliffs. Note the formation of the river bed beyond the gorge. Half a mile further, in wild moorland surroundings, the river makes a right-angled turn and can be seen coming down from Baugh Fell in a ravine. This is Rawthey Gill and it is two miles long at an easy gradient. The river has now dwindled to a stream but is no less charming; it is a chattering but captivating companion. Persist along the floor of the gill in confined surroundings, keeping generally on the west bank of the stream. At long last, after bypassing a waterfall, and beyond a sheepfold, the gill opens out. Take the west branch at the next confluence and climb alongside the infant Rawthey to its silent birthplace in the peat on the sprawling top of Baugh Fell. Go across to the summit wall, now in sight ahead, and follow it, right, to the Ordnance column (S 5662) on Knoutberry Haw, the highest point of the walk, thank goodness.

The environs of Rawthey Bridge, backed by the Howgill Fells, can now be seen, far far away. Return to it along the very wide shoulder extending for a full mile northwards with little loss of height; at its end a welcome view of Uldale opens up. Visit West Baugh Fell Tarn, which is easily passed unnoticed in spite of its size, before starting the long descent to Rawthey Bridge. Keep well above the trench of the river, trending northwest down an easy gradient. In the shallow depression before Bluecaster note a series of shakeholes as limestone is again reached. If sufficient energy remains, make a beeline up and over the top of Bluecaster to Rawthey Bridge, but if flesh and blood can take no more climbing, stagger down the gentle slope on the right to rejoin the path used on the outward journey.

If time is not pressing (as it is likely to be) and a reserve of strength can be called upon (which is most unlikely) a more interesting route of return may be made by leaving the north shoulder earlier between two shepherds' cairns and heading straight down the moor to the dark ravine of Taythes Gill below. Visit the waterfall (a miniature Gordale Scar), noting the weird limestone formations produced by erosion in the gorge nearby; then keep on the east bank down the ravine, rounding it at the foot to cross easy slopes to the old Bluecaster road, which, if followed to the right, leads unerringly down to Rawthey Bridge. You will be glad to see it again, especially so if the car is still there.

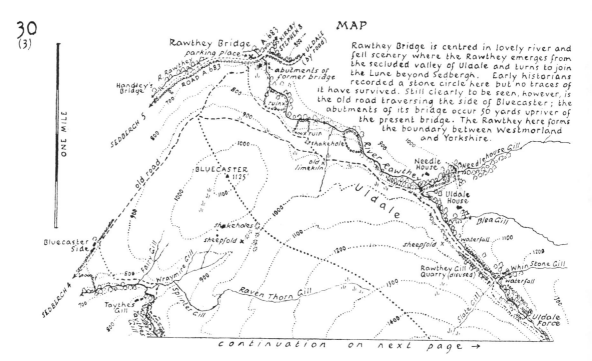

MAP

Rawthey Bridge is centred in lovely river and fell scenery where the Rawthey emerges from the secluded valley of Uldale and turns to join the Lune beyond Sedbergh. Early historians recorded a stone circle here but no traces of it have survived. Still clearly to be seen, however, is the old road traversing the side of Bluecaster; the abutments of its bridge occur 50 yards upriver of the present bridge. The Rawthey here forms the boundary between Westmorland and Yorkshire.

Rawthey Bridge
parking place
abutments of former bridge
ruins
R Rawthey
Handley's Bridge
ROAD A 683
SEDBERGH 5
old road
ruin
shakehole
River Rawthey
old limekiln
BLUECASTER
1125
Needle House
Needlehouse Gill
Uldale House
Uldale
Blea Gill
shakeholes
sheepfold
waterfall
sheepfold
Bluecaster Side
Fairy Gill
Wraymire Gill
Spinter Gill
Rawthey Gill Quarry (disused)
Whin Stone Gill
waterfall
Slate Gill
SEDBERGH 4
Raven Thorn Gill
Taythes Gill
Gills
Uldale Force

ONE MILE

continuation on next page →

MAP

30
(4)

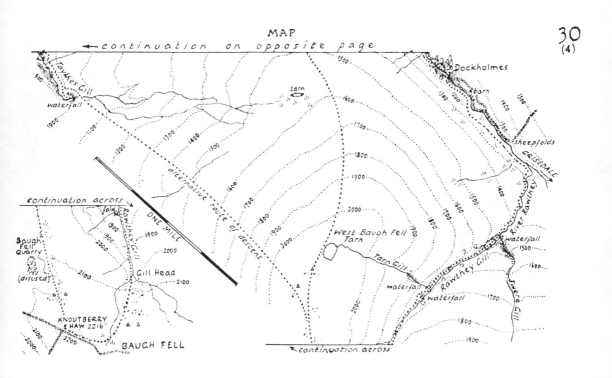

← continuation on opposite page

Tavkes Gill

900

waterfall

1000

1100

1200

1300

1400

1500

1600

tarn

1500

1600

1700

1800

1900

2000

Dockholmes

barn

1800

1700

1600

1500

1400

1300

sheepfolds

GRISEDALE

1400

1500

River Rawthey

alternative route of descent

continuation across

old

Rawthey Gill

ONE MILE

Baugh
Fell
Quarry

(disused)

1800

1900

2000

2000

2100

2100

Gill Head

West Baugh Fell Tarn

Tarn Gill

waterfall

1900

1800

1700

1600

1500

Rawthey Gill

waterfall

1500

1600

1700

1800

1900

Sedbe Gill

waterfall

2000

KNOUTBERRY HAW 2216'

2100

2200

2200

2000

2000

BAUGH FELL

← continuation across

Uldale Force

Waterfall on the River Rawthey

The limestone gorge of Dockholmes

The summit of Knoutberry Haw

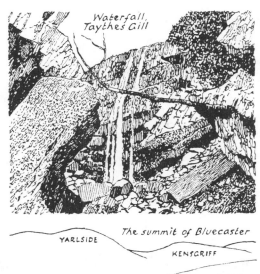

Waterfall, Taythes Gill

There is a West Baugh Fell and an East Baugh Fell. Knoutberry Haw, the apex of the West Fell, has a massive summit wall running across it with a column of the Ordnance Survey alongside but otherwise is a featureless rounded hump. The name 'Knoutberry' is a local one for cloudberry and this is one of the few places in the area where the plant is to be found. The view of the Howgills, seen from end to end, is good, as is the prospect over the vale of Sedbergh. Wild Boar Fell overtops Swarth Fell, northeast. Southwards both Penyghent and Whernside are seen but Ingleborough is conspicuous by its absence, being hidden by Whernside. But the overriding impression is the extensiveness of the top of Baugh Fell — miles of it with little rise and fall. This must be a bad place in mist, and it is well to remember in such conditions that the wall, followed west, is a perfect guide to Garsdale Foot, civilisation and tarmac roads.

The summit of Bluecaster

YARLSIDE

KENSGRIFF

WANDALE HILL

This is the simplest way up Baugh Fell, the route
being uncomplicated and foolproof even in mist
but also tedious and uninteresting. It starts
and finishes in pleasant scenery.

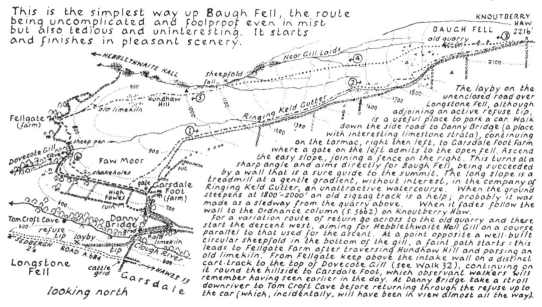

The layby on the
unenclosed road over
Longstone Fell, although
adjoining an active refuse tip,
is a useful place to park a car. Walk
down the side road to Danny Bridge (a place
with interesting limestone strata), continuing
on the tarmac, right then left, to Garsdale Foot Farm
where a gate on the left admits to the open fell. Ascend
the easy slope, joining a fence on the right. This turns at a
sharp angle and aims directly for Baugh Fell, being succeeded
by a wall that is a sure guide to the summit. The long slope is a
treadmill at a gentle gradient, without interest, in the company of
Ringing Keld Gutter, an unattractive watercourse. When the ground
steepens at 1800'-2000' an old zigzag track is a help; probably it was
made as a sledway from the quarry above. When it fades follow the
wall to the Ordnance column (S.5662) on Knoutberry Haw.
  For a variation route of return go across to the old quarry and there
start the descent west, aiming for Hebblethwaite Hall Gill on a course
parallel to that used for the ascent. At a point opposite a well-built
circular sheepfold in the bottom of the gill, a faint path starts: this
leads to Fellgate Farm after traversing Hundhaw Hill and passing an
old limekiln. From Fellgate keep above the intake wall on a distinct
cart track to the top of Dovecote Gill (see Walk 32), continuing on
it round the hillside to Garsdale Foot, which observant walkers will
remember having seen earlier in the day. At Danny Bridge take a stroll
downriver to Tom Croft Cave before returning through the refuse up to
the car (which, incidentally, will have been in view almost all the way).

looking north

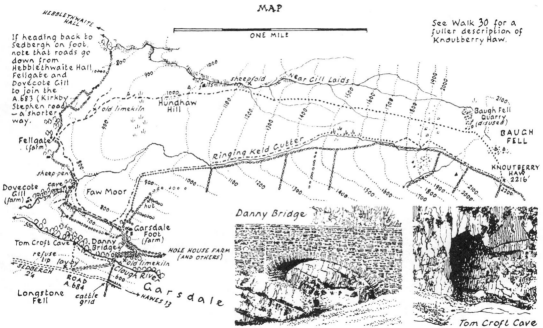

ONE MILE

31
(2)

See Walk 30 for a fuller description of Knoutberry Haw.

HEBBLETHWAITE HALL

If heading back to Sedbergh on foot, note that roads go down from Hebblethwaite Hall, Fellgate and Dovecote Gill to join the A.683 (Kirkby Stephen road — a shorter way.

old limekiln

Hundhaw Hill

Fellgate (farm)

a. falls

sheepfold

Near Gill Laids

Baugh Fell Quarry (disused)

BAUGH FELL b.a.

Ringing Keld Cutter

KNOUTBERRY HAW 2216'

sheep pen

Dovecote cave Gill (farm)

Faw Moor

hut

Garsdale Foot (farm)

Tom Croft Cave

refuse tip lay-by

SEDBERGH 2¾

Danny Bridge

HOLE HOUSE FARM (AND OTHERS)

old limekiln

Clough River

ROAD A.684

cattle grid

Longstone Fell

Garsdale

HAWES 13

Danny Bridge

Tom Croft Cave

Burntmill Bridge

A recent road improvement has left an obsolete loop at Burntmill Bridge convenient for parking a car. Take the narrow lane nearby, signposted 'Dowbiggin' and enjoy its flowery hedges until Dovecote Gill Farm is reached, then proceed through the wooded gill beyond, as detailed on the opposite page. From the top of the ravine use cart-tracks to cross the open moor above the intake walls to the beginnings of Hebblethwaite Hall Gill, which follow down on the far bank, noting a cave in the sharp bend of the ravine, to the plank bridge over Nor Gill. The scenery here is very lovely: the setting is spectacular and yet sylvan, the deeply-incurred stream cascading between rocks under a bower of trees.   A good track now goes forward to Hebblethwaite Hall, whence a road descends to the A.683, but when it turns sharp right a footpath indicated by stiles goes through fields to Ghyllas and continues in the same line to the road, descending to the verge in a flight of steps.

Dovecote Cave is the sort of place that
makes an old man feel young again!

A visit to two charming
limestone ravines.
This is a walk
in Arcadia.

looking north

An area of disused coal mines

Hebblethwaite Hall (farms)

KIRKBY STEPHEN 12

River Rowthey   A.683

farm road

Nor Gill

gate   gates

hurdle   gate   ruin

falls   Cave   fall

Hebblethwaite Hall Gill

600   700   900

Ghyllas

stile   stiles   600   pastures

Straight Bridge

Burntmill Bridge   Dowbiggin

500

old limekiln
Surface limestone again (a green patch on the moor). A series of shakeholes, some used as charnel-pits.

Fellgate (farm)

Wilkinstile

SEDBERGH 1½   A.683

Dowbiggin Lane

400   500   2ᴹ   3   4 FELLGATE   600   pastures

Note here the sudden change from limestone to sandstone, and its effect on the scenery. Geologically, we are on the edge of the Dent Fault.

1   5   6   7

sheep pens

Dovecote Gill (farm)   Dovecote Gill

DOWBIGGIN HOMESTEADS
1: Dowbiggin Foot
2: Kilnbeck
3: Gate Side
4: Greenwood
5: Green Hollins
6: Broad Yeat
7: Spout

gate   stile   footbridge (don't use it)

MAP

32
(2)

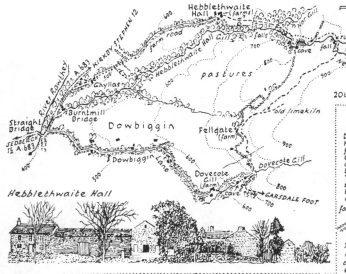

Hebblethwaite Hall — (farm)

KIRKBY STEPHEN 12

600

farm road

Hebblethwaite Hall Gill

600

falls

Nor Gill

x ruin

cave

fall

Far Gill Laids

700

p a s t u r e s

800

900

Near Gill Laids

River Rawthey   A 683

Ghyllas

Burntmill Bridge

Straight Bridge

SEDBERGH 1½ A 683

400

500

D o w b i g g i n

Fellgate (farm)

old limekiln

900

Dowbiggin Lane

600

Dowbiggin

500

Dovecote Gill (farm)

Dovecote Gill

800

cave

600   700

GARSDALE FOOT

ONE MILE

There is an interesting cluster of buildings at Hebblethwaite Hall with 17th. century features. A mill was established in the 18th. century for the manufacture of woollen goods (and later, bobbins). 20th. century activity is confined to farming.

DOVECOTE GILL AND CAVE

Do not cross the footbridge. Keep high by the fence for 200 yards, then trend down into the gill. Track the stream up to the cave.

FELLGATE

stream enters four eyeholes old limekiln

stream issues

From the upper cave climb up to a wall on the right and follow it down to a stile.

stile

x ruin

farm   gate

fence

fence

footbridge

GARSDALE FOOT

100 yards

The lower cave (where the stream issues) is hidden round a corner and reached by a rough scramble over boulders. It can be entered and followed underground (100 yards) to the upper cave (a fine chamber where the stream enters in a waterfall). A series of eyeholes admits daylight to the subterranean passage. These are seen on the overland journey, the last one having a cave-like opening giving easy access to the chamber of the upper cave.

Hebblethwaite Hall

NOTE — Dovecote Gill and Cave are on PRIVATE land and there is NO public right of way to them. Because of recent damage admission is now prohibited unless you get consent at the farm. There is, however, a public path from the farm direct to Fellgate.

Penny Farm Gill,
leading to
Hebblethwaite Hall Gill.

Dovecote Cave
— the lower
entrance

READER'S PERSONAL LOG

This and the next three pages are designed
for the use of readers who may wish to keep
a personal record of their performance of
the walks listed in the book.

Walk	Date	Time start	Time finish	Companions	Weather
1					
2					
3					
4					
5					
6					
7					

Walk	Date	Time		Companions	Weather
		start	finish		
8					
9					
10					
11					
12					
13					
14					
15					
16					
17					

Walk	Date	Time		Companions	Weather
		start	finish		
18					
19					
20					
21					
22					
23					
24					
25					
26					
27					

Walk	Date	Time		Companions	Weather
		start	finish		
28					
29					
30					
31					
32					

One inch to a mile Ordnance Survey maps covering the area of this book:

NO. 89 : KENDAL AND LANCASTER   No. 90 : WENSLEYDALE
and a very small section of No. 83 : PENRITH (so small that it isn't worth buying)

Photographs by the author

The Lune Gorge, from Fairmile Road

Borrow Beck, Borrowdale

The summit of Winder

Sedbergh, from the slopes of Winder

The head of Langdale

Bowderdale

The Calf, from Calders

Baugh Fell, Rawthey valley and Garsdale

The Howgill Fells, from Firbank

The Howgill Fells, from Frostrow

Hobdale and the Rawthey valley

Springtime in the Rawthey valley

Wild Boar Fell, from Knott

The escarpment, Wild Boar Fell

Grisedale Pike, Baugh Fell

SYMBOLS AND ABBREVIATIONS USED IN THE MAPS

Good footpath (sufficiently distinct to be followed in mist)

Intermittent footpath (difficult to follow in mist)

No path; route recommended

Walking routes given in this book are not necessarily rights of way

Route on motor road   unenclosed   between walls   between fences

Unenclosed road (off route)

Wall   Broken wall   Fence   Broken fence

Limestone clints   Crags   Scree   Boulders

Marshy ground   Trees

Cave or pothole •   Buildings   Contours (at 100' intervals) ....1400.... ....1300....

Summit-cairn ▲   Other (prominent) cairns △   Miles (from starting point) and direction of route ⑤

Stream or river (arrow indicates direction of flow)

Waterfall   Bridge   Railway   Map scale: 2" = 1 mile North is top of the page

Abbreviations: O.S. Ordnance Survey   Y.H.A Youth Hostels Association